D0450441

"Carmen is so unflinchingl‹ ing her memoir reminds me of how impossible it is for her to be anything else! She recounts the unthinkable events that changed her life with brave authenticity. Even though I know her story, I'm still moved to tears—not just by the tragedy, but also by her unrelenting march toward restoration and normalcy. Carmen was and is determined not just to survive but triumph over her circumstances. I suspect most of us are made of much weaker stuff, which is why we need a Carmen in our lives! She is one of the most resilient people I know, and her journey has given her a unique perspective about what matters and what doesn't. She doesn't try to be inspirational—she just is. *Overcome: Burned, Blinded, and Blessed* is an opportunity to bask, for just for a little while, in the rays of her exceptional spirit. Don't miss it!"

JONI BUSBY
SUPERVISING PRODUCER, *THE DOCTORS*

"Carmen's story is one of tragedy and triumph. She is truly an example of the strength and beauty of the human spirit. Carmen went from victim to survivor and teaches us all that we can overcome the unimaginable and create the lives we would like to live."

JENNIFER RADICS, MBA
EXECUTIVE DIRECTOR, ALISA ANN RUCH BURN FOUNDATION

"Carmen Tarleton's story is a riveting account of a courageous woman who teaches us all the power of fighting suffering with relentless hope and tenacity."

SAMIR MELKI, MD, PhD
FOUNDER, BOSTON EYE GROUP

"Carmen tells her inspiring story with remarkable clarity and honesty. She has endured a journey many might be unable to endure and arrived to provide the reader with wisdom, compassion, and inspiration. As heavy as the price was for Carmen, *Overcome* is a wonderful gift to those of us who take the time to read it. Her story is, at heart, one of a profound and courageous journey, and she has arrived with great treasures to offer us all."

DAVID VOGEL
PRESIDENT, BURN SURVIVORS OF NEW ENGLAND

"Told with sincerity and grace, *Overcome* powerfully illustrates the unlimited resilience of the human spirit. Carmen's heart-thumping journey is at times harrowing, yet always keenly illuminating. *Overcome* is a bracing triumph of the soul."

MICHAEL PAUL MASON
AUTHOR OF *HEAD CASES: STORIES OF BRAIN INJURY AND ITS AFTERMATH*

OVERCOME: BURNED, BLINDED, AND BLESSED

Copyright © 2013 Carmen Blandin Tarleton

All rights reserved. Except as permitted under the
U.S. Copyright Act of 1976, no part of this publication may
be reproduced, distributed, or transmitted in any form or by
any means, or stored in a database or retrieval system,
without the prior written permission of the publisher.

Writers of the Round Table Press
PO Box 511, Highland Park, IL 60035

*RTC Publishing is an imprint of Writers of the Round Table, Inc.
Writers of the Round Table Press and the RTC Publishing logo
are trademarks of Writers of the Round Table, Inc.*

Publisher and Executive Editor: Corey Michael Blake
Editor: Katie Gutierrez
Creative Director, Post Production, Digital Publishing: David Charles Cohen
Cover Photography: Ben Hood
Front Cover Design: Analee Paz
Interior Design and Layout, Back Cover: Sunny DiMartino
Proofreading: Rita Hess
Last Looks: Aaron Hierholzer
Directoress of Happiness: Erin Cohen
Coordinator of Chaos: Kristin Westberg
Facts Keeper: Mike Winicour

Printed in the United States of America

First Edition: February 2013
10   9   8   7   6   5   4   3   2   1

Library of Congress Cataloging-in-Publication Data
Tarleton, Carmen Blandin
Overcome: Burned, Blinded, and Blessed / Carmen Blandin Tarleton.–
1st ed. p. cm.
ISBN 978-1-939418-11-1   EISBN 978-1-939418-12-8
Library of Congress Control Number: 2013932309

This book is based upon actual events, persons, and experiences. Several
of the characters' names have been changed to protect their privacy. Any
similarity to the name attributes or actual background of any actual person,
living or dead, other than those in the author's history, is entirely coincidental.
Additionally, scenes, dialogue, and description have been truthfully
reconstructed from memory; any inaccuracies are completely unintentional.

OVERCOME

∘ ∘ ∘

BURNED,
BLINDED,
AND
BLESSED

CARMEN BLANDIN TARLETON

CONTENTS

ACKNOWLEDGMENTS

I would like to give a special thanks to my Round Table Companies team: Katie, Corey, Erin, David, Kristin, and Ben. This book would not have been possible without your help.

Thank you to my community. The Upper Valley holds so many special and caring people who showed me their goodness when I needed it most.

To my friends, old and new, thank you. Bill and Kathie, Tonya, Sally, and many others—you eased my burden during a hard time. I am especially grateful to Eileen for having the courage to stand beside me when her own life was difficult.

I am enormously grateful for my family. To my sister, Kess; my mom and dad; my brother, Don, and sister-in-law, Jeanie—you gave me what I needed to move forward at my own speed. I can't thank you enough for being by my side.

Thank you to the many doctors, nurses, and other health professionals who helped me along the way. You are heroic.

Lastly, thank you to my daughters, Liza and Hannah. Life challenged us greatly, and you two rose to it. I am so grateful for your genuine compassion and love. I love you both very much.

CHAPTER 1

THE BRIGHT AND UNKNOWABLE FUTURE

WHEN YOU ARE YOUNG, YOU ARE WILLING TO DO almost anything for the experience; at least, I was. At twenty-eight years old, I loaded up my station wagon with everything I needed for a cross-country adventure: clothing, dishes, my kids' toys, photo albums. It was time for a change. With my two young daughters, I left the Upper Valley region of Vermont and New Hampshire to build a new life in Los Angeles.

After the small towns I'd called home my whole life, everything about LA overwhelmed me: the soaring buildings, labyrinthine highways, thick and crawling traffic. I lived with a friend of my sister's before renting a small furnished apartment. The only routes I knew were to and from the grocery store, work, and the park. I also learned through trial and error not to go anywhere mid-afternoon.

Once, at three thirty, I decided to take little Liza and Hannah to a kids' furniture store on Olympic Boulevard. It was a straight shot from my place, I thought; no way to get lost. It turned out the boulevard stretched from Santa

Monica, where I lived, to Beverly Hills. With four-year-old Liza and two-year-old Hannah belted into their seats, I got caught in lanes choked with traffic. Brake lights glared from every side street. I'd never experienced this trapped feeling before, and my body prickled with sweat.

It took an hour to travel eight or nine miles, and traffic still swirled in every direction when I found the furniture store. Parallel parking was not an option in my bulky station wagon, and I couldn't walk far with two small children. My heart pounded as I circled unfamiliar streets, trying to remember the way back to the store and then home. Finally, I happened upon a parking spot along a side street and gratefully unloaded the girls from the car.

The furniture store, where we bought side-by-side beds that could eventually be converted to bunk beds, was a brief reprieve. The drive back home in peak-hour traffic took even longer than the original trip, and my neck was tight with anxiety when I returned.

My older sister, Kess, who had moved to LA a few months earlier, sympathized with my stress. "It takes some time to get used to all this," she said. "At least you have a job."

I had been a registered nurse in New Hampshire, and the hospital where I worked had recently announced that it was laying off forty nurses. If people left voluntarily, the layoffs wouldn't be as severe. As incentive, the hospital—Mary Hitchcock Memorial—offered a handsome severance package that paid four months' salary and maintained benefits for six months. I had worked there for almost eight years. I wasn't afraid of losing my job, but it hit me that maybe I could take that severance package and leave. Nurses could find work anywhere, and with Kess's recent move to LA, I immediately thought of UCLA. It was one of the top hospitals in the country, and I couldn't help idealizing it. More importantly, I had lived in the Upper Valley my whole life; this might be my only opportunity to leave.

Before taking the leap, I had to talk to my ex-husband. Brian had left his hometown in his twenties, so he would understand the impulse. However, if he intended to be a big part of our daughters' lives, I would stay; leaving wasn't important enough to take the girls from their father without his consent. As it turned out, he said, "Go ahead."

His answer saddened me; if roles were reversed, I wouldn't want him taking them from me. At the same time, I felt fortunate for the chance to do something different, something for me. By September of 1996, I had a job at UCLA.

My heart beat fast and heavy with anxiety during those first six months, but I was also happy. I felt free. I couldn't believe I had actually done it, and I walked into UCLA feeling euphoric, as though I had *accomplished* something.

Nursing school had been an intuitive choice—I was nineteen and working at a convenience store when I decided to learn a trade. I had no idea what a nurse actually did, but I liked working with people. It was what I most enjoyed about working at the store. During snowstorms, I rose early and opened at five in the morning, making coffee for the cold-reddened snowplow men. When I enrolled in LPN school, I discovered that there was a special camaraderie in nursing, a social aspect to shared caregiving. The career seemed like a fit for me.

Once I started working, I discovered I had a strong intuition: I could always tell when someone was going to die. Blood pressure could be fine, heart rate fine, blood work fine, but sometimes something felt ... off. Sure enough, later, the patient would crash. I didn't contemplate it the way I do now, but there is a certain sacredness about the spirit, the life force, that leaves the body the instant it stops working. I was attuned to that energy and volunteered often for postmortem duties. I wanted to take care of the body left behind because I knew I could do it respectfully.

Despite the unity I enjoyed with other nurses, I tried to do this part of my job alone. Once I was sure no family was returning to say their goodbyes, I removed whatever tubes were threaded in the patient's throat, arms, or hands and spoke to that person in my mind: *I know you had a good life*, I'd think at him. *Your wife told me about your vacation last Christmas* ... I carefully bathed the body and slipped a clean hospital gown and blankets around it. I made sure the right name and hospital number were written on the patient's toe tag and tied it to the big toe before shrouding the body in a bag. Then I attached another tag to the outside zipper, left the room, and closed the door. The transportation team would arrive later with a discreet gurney to wheel the body to the morgue.

Those were sacred times to me, but I didn't impose my feelings on those who didn't think the same way. If another nurse was helping me clean a body and telling me about her date Friday night, I just listened. The respect I felt wasn't about religion, like when I had gone to church with my grandmother years back, so it wasn't open to offense. It was about the spirit I used to feel in the woods as a kid, with my dog—something wordless, strong, and sweet—and I felt those moments again when I was around dead and dying people.

The intuition I developed as a nurse served me well in my career. I made good money on a per-diem rate at UCLA. The hardship came when my severance package was about to expire—meaning no insurance for the kids. In December of 1996, my boss at UCLA asked me to take a fulltime position with benefits. I took a huge pay cut but accepted. When our six-month apartment lease was up, I found another, significantly cheaper, apartment and moved the three of us in.

Being a single mother didn't weigh heavily on me. I had known from a young age that I wanted kids and would be responsible for them—end of story. Not that it was easy. Soon, between childcare, rent, and other living expenses, I was barely getting by. There were times I had to borrow money from Kess to buy groceries. It was hard, but at least I was on my own, and the kids didn't know the difference. They were young and happy. The uphill battle of starting over had to end some time.

° ° °

In 1998, I'd been working at UCLA for two years. I had made friends—Aileen, Joyce, Tina—and on rare nights away from my girls, we tried new restaurants and went dancing at clubs. One Halloween, Aileen took me down to the West Hollywood Gay Halloween Street Parade. Dressed as a genie, I laughed and danced and marveled at the outrageous costumes along with hundreds of thousands of other spectators. The warm California evening pulsed with energy; it was like nothing I'd ever experienced before.

Around that time, I had my first real conversation with Herbert Rodgers. Herb, as everyone called him, was one of the guys we nurses called when patients needed some kind of equipment—a walker, an oxygen tank, a special kind of bed—and he was always friendly and flexible. I'd spoken to him now and then over the course of the last year, but not much more than a smile and a "Hi, how are you?"

One day, late that summer, a group of us was gathered in the cardiac monitor room at UCLA. It was my job to watch the rhythmic blips of the machines, and Herb came in and joined the conversation we were having at the workstation. Someone mentioned baking, and Herb piped up, saying he made pound cake from scratch.

"Oh, yeah?" I said with a smile. "I love sweets."

"Is that right?" Herb replied. "How about I make you a pound cake and bring it in on Tuesday?"

I caught our colleagues trading glances, and sure enough, I got a few joking comments later in the day along the lines of, "Ooh, Herb likes Carmen!"

As it turned out, I didn't make it to work on Tuesday. Hannah and Liza—now almost four and six years old—had gone on a Labor Day trip to the Santa Monica Mountains with my sister, and they returned with two raging cases of poison ivy. I had to miss the whole week of work to take care of them.

When I ran into Herb in the hallway the next week, he was picking up the plate he'd used to bring the pound cake. I apologized for missing his homemade cake, but I could tell he had taken it personally.

"It's fine," he said, brushing past me without making eye contact.

Oh, well, I thought. *He just doesn't understand what it's like to have kids.*

After that, I didn't see Herb for a month or so. He was always working for a different medical equipment company. Something would go wrong with one company and Herb would move on to a new one, so it wasn't too strange to not see him for a while.

One day in October, I'd taken the girls up to UCLA so Hannah could get all her shots, and there in the elevator was Herb. He greeted me warmly, and the girls, feeling shy, hid behind me. Hannah peeked out from behind my leg.

"I got a shot today," she ventured. "I didn't even cry!"

"Wow!" Herb bent closer to Hannah, a proud smile breaking across his face. "Good for you!"

"Hey, Herb," I said, "I'm really sorry about missing that pound cake."

He was much more open this time. "Oh no, it's okay," he said. "Sounds like these little girls needed their mom. I totally understand."

I figured his manly pride had been hurt the first time, and now that he'd met the girls, he understood I hadn't blown him off on purpose. We had a short but pleasant conversation after that, and I left the hospital thinking we might go on a date soon. I'd started to like Herb. At forty-three, he was thirteen years older than I was, but there was a gentleness about him that attracted me.

Herb soon changed companies again, and this time it was like he'd dropped off the face of the earth. I was disappointed, so about a month later I decided to see what I could do about it. My friend Donna worked the front desk at UCLA, and she was the type who knew everything about everyone.

I marched down to reception. "Hey, Donna, you know Herb, right?" I asked, casually resting an elbow on her desk.

"Yeah, of course," she said. "I've known him for, what … over ten years now."

"Do me a favor, Donna. Next time you see him, get his number for me," I said with a mischievous smile.

Donna snickered. "You got it, Carmen."

As expected, Donna came through for me. By the next Wednesday, she had run into Herb and asked for his number. I thanked Donna profusely and called Herb the next night.

"Hello, it's Carmen," I said, smiling. "As you know, I asked Donna for your number."

To my surprise, his voice was gruff. "Yeah, I know. I gave it to her on Monday. What took you so long to call?"

"I didn't see her," I said, taken aback. "I only work three days a week."

"Oh." His voice changed, softened. "Right. I understand. So … do you want to go out to lunch this week?"

For just a moment, I hesitated. His initial roughness had turned me off, but I was still interested in him. "That sounds great," I said finally. "But I'm going to have to bring Hannah with me."

Liza was already in school, but Hannah was still at home during the day. I was reluctant to tell Herb about our third wheel, but he'd met the girls in the elevator, after all, and he knew my ex-husband lived in Vermont and wasn't a big part of my life.

To my relief, he said, "That's fine with me."

We agreed to meet at a restaurant in Culver City, and I embarked on my due diligence as a modern woman:

asking around about him. No one—from acquaintances to his supervisor—had anything bad to say. The small amount of unease I felt as a single mother had been assuaged. It was now time to tell Hannah about our lunch plans.

"Hannah, honey, you and I are going to have lunch with my friend Herb tomorrow," I said. "How does that sound?"

Hannah stared up at me with her huge, irresistible four-year-old eyes. "Is that your boyfriend?"

"No, baby, he's just a friend."

Hannah thought it over for a moment. "Can I wear my yellow dress?"

I told her of course she could, and the next day we spent close to an hour getting her all dolled up for the date. Hannah was thrilled at the chance to wear her favorite outfit and insisted that her ponytail be just so. I, on the other hand, a tomboy at heart, did my version of dressing up: I made sure I had clean clothes and combed hair.

We met Herb at the restaurant and picked out a table on the patio. It was a gorgeous, mild November day in Culver City. Though I rarely allowed the girls to drink soda, this day felt special, so I let Hannah—looking beyond cute in her radiant yellow dress—order a Coke from the waiter.

"Hannah picked her outfit especially for today," I said to Herb.

He took the hint. Smiling at my little girl, he said, "You look very pretty today, Hannah."

She beamed back. As Herb and I talked, Hannah entertained herself, repeatedly picking up her cup, taking a sip from the straw, and setting it down. She was adorably well behaved, interjecting in the conversation only when we spoke to her.

That day, I felt myself growing close to Herb, even though I still knew little about him. I desperately wanted a second chance at a serious relationship, and here was a thoughtful, hardworking, gentle man who was interested in me—a divorced mother of two. I'd dated other guys after divorcing Brian two years earlier, but I was tired of having a fling here, a little sex there. I was ready to move on, to have a real relationship.

Herb seemed ready for a second chance of his own. He'd had a son when he was eighteen and was estranged from most of his family. It was a situation I understood all too well. My family was deeply reserved and independent; everyone lived their own lives.

Eventually, after our plates had been cleared, Hannah spoke up and said she had to go to the bathroom. I took her inside, and when we came back, the date ended. Though it had only lasted an hour—a normal span for lunch, especially with a toddler—I was excited. I liked Herb. I wanted him to ask me out again.

That afternoon, when Liza got home from school, Hannah's delight at our lunch date hadn't faded. Liza was curious and felt a little left out, but I assured her that she would get to see Herb before long.

Liza got her chance soon enough. After our date with Hannah, Herb and I talked on the phone often. One night, I gave Herb a call and said, "Gosh, Herb, it's getting cold and I have no idea how to light the little furnace in this apartment."

"Why don't I come over and see if I can fix it?" he said.

"Think you could?"

"I can't get over there until eight thirty or so, but I can give it a try."

That night, I put the girls in bed at the normal time, around eight o'clock. As I tucked them in and gave them their goodnight kisses, I let them know that Herb was coming by to look at the furnace, so if they heard someone, that's who it was. I should have known better than to think Liza would resist the temptation to catch a peek.

Herb arrived a while later and quickly set to work trying to light the furnace. As I watched him struggle, crouched on all fours next to the couch, I heard the girls' door creak open down the hall. Liza and Hannah, dressed in their pajamas, shuffled into the living room, directing wide-eyed stares at the visitor. Liza—full of curiosity, just like her mother—climbed on the couch to observe Herb up close.

Herb, realizing he had an audience, sat up and gave the girls a shy wave.

"Liza," I said, "this is Herb. Herb, this is Liza."

"Hi," Liza said, still staring at Herb.

"Hi," Herb replied.

I could tell that Herb was nervous as he fumbled to light the match. I was nervous, too. I was falling for him, and I wondered how he would get along with the girls. I knew firsthand how hard being a stepparent could be; leaving my ex-husband's sons had been very difficult for me—more difficult than leaving my husband himself.

"Girls, give him some space," I laughed. They were both staring at him from the couch.

"I'm up here, Mommy," Liza said from her perch. "It's okay."

After the girls had gaped at Herb a little longer, I sent them back to their room. Herb labored valiantly at the furnace for a few minutes longer, but he didn't have any more luck than I'd had.

"Looks like I can't fix it," he said sheepishly. "You'll have to call the gas company tomorrow."

I could tell he'd hoped to come in as the man and give heat to my kids and me. Despite his embarrassment, we enjoyed each other's company, chatting for a few more minutes before he left.

As fall turned to winter, Herb and I saw more and more of each other. Soon we were together nearly every day and calling each other on the days we weren't. Almost everything we did was centered around the girls. He'd come over and play with them and then cook dinner for us. Hannah and Liza climbed him like a tree, and he took off his glasses so they could crawl over his head and stand on his shoulders.

Months after our first date, we were sitting together on the living room couch and Hannah took his arm. She tapped his skin.

"Oh, you're black," she said, as if she had just noticed.

Herb looked at me as we both laughed. "Yes, I am."

The moment passed, and we stayed up late as we usually did after the girls went to bed. I asked him every nosy question known to man: had he ever had any diseases, taken IV drugs, hit a woman? These were the questions, said my city friends, a woman—especially a mother—should ask a new man she dated. Herb answered them all without hesitation: "No," he said. When I asked about his family, he told me his first marriage had been dysfunctional. He moved to California in 1976, at twenty-one years old.

"I wanted a new start," he said. "I didn't like who I was before."

Herb didn't go into much detail about his past, but that was okay; I didn't expect him to relate to me as openly as a girlfriend. I also didn't hold his younger-man mistakes against him; we all made mistakes. The truth was that it wouldn't have mattered what he told me. Nothing could have changed my emotions. I was falling in love.

Six months after our patio date with Hannah, Herb and I were still growing closer every day. We talked frequently about moving in together, but one thing struck me as odd: while he had become a fixture at my apartment, I had never seen his place. Not even once.

"Am I ever going to get to see where you live, Herb?" I asked him one night after the girls had been ushered off to bed. I knew he lived in a one-bedroom apartment but that a friend of his stayed on the couch.

He looked down at the ground. "I've actually got a big problem with you seeing it."

"Why?"

"Because it's a mess."

"Everyone's place gets messy, Herb. I don't care."

He lifted his gaze to mine. "No, I mean it's *really* a mess. It's gross. I've been to therapy to figure out why I keep doing this, why I keep not picking up after myself. But it hasn't helped."

I didn't know what to say. "Can I see it?" I asked after a few moments of tense silence.

"I feel like I need you to see it. I'm just not ready yet."

A couple of weeks later, Herb called me at home. "Okay," he said. "I think it's time you came to my apartment."

I knew where he lived—I passed it every day on my way to work. His apartment complex was in a firmly middle-class, commercial part of town. A bank and other

13

small businesses surrounded it. When I parked, Herb was waiting for me outside. I walked over to where he stood, looking very much on edge.

"I'm shaking, Carmen," he said.

I glanced down at his trembling hands. "Why?"

"I'm afraid you won't want to be with me if you see this. But I've got to show it to you."

When I walked into the dark, sparse apartment, I was floored. I stood in silence in the gloom, glancing from the dingy walls to the tattered couch. A black path on the carpet traced a route from the couch to the kitchen. In the bathroom, I found a toilet bowl blackened with rings. The filthy kitchen counters held a great big roast in a dirty pan; the roast looked eaten straight out of the pan, as if—animalistic—no one had bothered with a plate or utensils. All that remained were the bones and some hanging flesh.

Herb's bedroom, though slightly neater, was piled with clothes. I could tell the clean from the dirty only by the dryer sheet lying on one stack. His bed was a box spring and mattress on the floor, and the sheets looked as though they'd never been washed. I knew I would never sleep there. Part of me screamed, *Run!*

We didn't talk at all as we walked through the apartment. We left after a few minutes, getting in my car for a drive. On the road, I was still speechless.

"You're not saying much," Herb observed.

"I know. I just ... give me a few minutes."

As I drove, my shock at Herb's living conditions gradually gave way to admiration for what he had done. I realized how difficult it must have been for him, making himself vulnerable by showing me his apartment, risking our relationship to show me how he lived. *You've got big balls, buddy,* I thought. But I truly appreciated his effort.

"How did it get that way?" I asked at last.

"I don't know."

I gave him a few moments to elaborate, but he didn't. "Well, you have to promise me you won't live that way with me," I said. "I have kids, Herb. You know my place isn't always spick-and-span, but I can't tolerate that."

"Of course," said Herb. I could see relief wash over his face—I was still talking about our future.

"As long as you're aware of it and promise to keep it under control with me, I don't think it's a big problem," I said. "In fact, I think it was really big of you to show me that. Thank you."

Herb smiled for the first time that day, and I continued praising him for his bravery. I loved Herb, and I thought that if he could open himself up like that this early in our relationship, it was a good sign for the future. We could only grow from here.

CHAPTER 2

NEWLYWEDS

A YEAR AFTER HERB AND I STARTED DATING, WE were still very much in love. He had been living with the girls and me for six months, and true to his word, his lifestyle in our apartment was nothing like it had been at his. While I didn't ask him to do housework—he didn't like it and wasn't good at it—he did his part for the family. He loved to cook, and each night he cheerfully prepared dinner for the kids and me. He made a delicious fried chicken, and we often brought home buffalo steaks from Whole Foods that he pan-fried. His meals were all stovetop; he didn't know how to bake except for cakes. He was always baking cakes: for the discharge planners and social workers at UCLA, for his customers, or for special events. The sweet smell of baked bread constantly filled our apartment.

In November of 1999, Herb said suddenly, "You know, if you wanted to, I would marry you tomorrow."

I had just told him that an acquaintance of ours was getting married, and his words, lifted with shy hope, shocked me. We were standing in the hallway, and at first, nothing came out of my mouth. Then I stuttered, "I—I can't get married. We can't get married right now."

Herb looked away, disappointedly pursing his lips. "Oh."

"I'm just not comfortable with that yet. And besides,"

I added, "I need you to pay all your back taxes first." Herb owed thousands to the IRS, and I couldn't join myself to him until the finances were clear. After all, I wanted to be able to buy a house together without fearing that the IRS would put liens on it. "That's my condition," I said.

"Okay. I understand."

"So … can we just keep doing what we're doing?"

"Yeah, Carmen. We can do that."

I could tell by the quietness of his voice that he was hurt. He had gone out on a limb, and I had left him there alone. But we had both been married and divorced. I never wanted to go through that pain again, nor did I want to drag Liza and Hannah through it. My first husband and I had married so quickly (we were engaged after four months!) that we didn't have the opportunity to fall in love over time. Instead, Brian and I had lived crisis to crisis, one major life event to the next. If I were ever to remarry, I needed to be as certain as one human could be that it was going to be for the rest of my life.

The next week, I overheard Herb on the phone in our bedroom. When I caught the word "taxes," I intentionally eavesdropped.

"I'm sorry," he said. "I've been five years without doing my taxes, but I got this great girl I want to marry, and she won't marry me until I take care of it. So what do I got to do?"

I smiled, full of love for him. Truth be told, I wanted to marry him, too. I was just scared.

Over the following year, as Herb paid off his back taxes, I grew not only deeper in love with him but also comfortable with our life together. The subject of marriage came up every so often. Eventually, my chest stopped clutching with the panic I'd felt when he first suggested it; instead, the idea made me smile.

November of 2000 brought our second anniversary. We were sitting on our living room couch after the girls were in bed, cuddling and talking quietly. That was when Herb tried again. "I know about a jeweler in downtown LA," he ventured. "I could get you a ring there."

This time, I smiled excitedly. After two years, most of which we had lived together, Herb knew what being with me was like beyond the initial infatuation. He knew I didn't cook and could be moody and say things I didn't mean. And he still wanted to be my husband and a father to Liza and Hannah.

"Well, I don't really care what kind of ring I have," I said, "as long as it isn't one of those with one big diamond in the middle." It was more than a style preference; I didn't want to have to twist my ring off every day when I made up hospital beds or did other manual tasks.

"So …," Herb said, starting to smile, "you want to get married?"

"Yeah. Do you want to get married?"

"Yeah!"

We laughed and hugged. Herb said he would design the ring and order it from the jeweler. We could go pick it up together when it came in.

"But I don't want to live in an apartment anymore," I said. "I want us to buy a house and get married in it."

Herb beamed. "Well, that sounds good to me."

My next step was to break our news to the girls. One day, when Herb wasn't home, I was playing in the living room with Liza and Hannah. "Girls," I said, "you know Herb and I have been together a long time. Well … we're going to get married."

Hannah, who was now six, hardly reacted; it was eight-year-old Liza who objected. She jumped up beside me on the couch and got right in my face. "Humph!" she said, little arms crossed. "Well, I don't want you to get married. I don't want you to have a husband. You can have a *boyfriend*!"

I tried not to laugh. "Honey—"

"You don't need a husband, Mom," she declared. "*I'll* be your husband!"

I pulled her to me and hid my smile in her hair. "I love you both so much," I told them. "Trust me. This is a good thing."

Later that evening, Liza gave me a note the way she did when she was upset. *Mom, I don't want you to marry Herd*, she wrote, endearingly spelling his name wrong. *Please marry me.*

I pressed my lips together, trying not to laugh when she was so serious. I sat with her that night, stroking her hair. "You know, Liza," I said, "Mommy's a grown woman. When you get older and fall in love, these things happen. You want to get married. Besides, it'll be good for us to have a man in the house to do things I can't necessarily do."

Liza looked at me skeptically with her big brown eyes.

"Really," I said. "This is a good thing."

Liza relented with a world-weary sigh. "*Okay*, Mommy."

In January of 2001, Herb made his final IRS payments; we were free to buy a house together. We looked at four or five places and ended up picking a 1940s fixer-upper in Hawthorne. Light streamed in through a great big window in the living room, and there was a fireplace I instantly envisioned sitting by in wintertime. Plus, the girls would have their own rooms, the house was in a good school district, and the price was right. I knew that with some attention—and the California market—we stood to make a profit in several years. In March, we moved in. Almost five years after coming out to California, I had done what I wanted to do: build a new life.

We planned our wedding for July. It was small with about twenty guests. Kess was there, along with my father, his girlfriend, and my friends from work. My mother and younger sister, Rachel, weren't able to fly out, and my brother had no interest. Herb, of course, was estranged from his family; he hadn't spoken to his mother, sister, or son in years.

The wedding cost almost nothing. Kess had bought me a little white dress, and my friends, who were of all different backgrounds, brought their favorite dishes. Frances came with her delicious homemade Chinese eggrolls, and Marina, who was Russian, brought home-made potato dumplings. The only things Herb and I paid for were the girls' dresses and the minister, whom we'd found through an advertisement. We paid less than five hundred dollars for the whole thing.

The afternoon was hot, so we held our one o'clock ceremony inside. We had picked vows for Herb to say to the girls, and when it came to that part, I stood back and let him speak. Repeating after the minister, he said earnestly, "Even though I'm marrying your mother, I want you to know that I'm here for you, too—that I love you, too, that you're a part of my life, too."

Liza was paying attention, but Hannah rocked back and forth, playing with the scarf around her neck. The vows were long, and after a few minutes, the kids stopped listening. Their eyes wandered around the room while Herb was sweating bullets in his tux, trying to make this commitment. I tried not to laugh. The kids were always so entertaining. Herb thought so, too.

By five, everyone was gone. My dad and his girlfriend, who were staying at a hotel in Santa Monica for the week, took the girls overnight. It was only the second night Herb and I had ever spent without the kids, and we went out to dinner at our favorite sushi restaurant. Then we came home and went to bed early. The next morning, we made love before we picked up the girls for our "family honeymoon" at Disneyland. I couldn't have been happier.

° ° °

Of course, not everything was perfect. Herb and I occasionally struck up against old issues and bickered the way every couple does. When we did argue—albeit infrequently—it seemed it was always for the same reason: Herb holding something insignificant back from me.

Before we were married, when we still lived in Culver City, he had built up a collection of parking tickets; traveling from hospital to hospital, with LA's terrible parking situation, it wasn't surprising. However, he was using my car. The registration was under my name. When he finally told me about the tickets—almost a thousand dollars' worth—I was floored.

"Don't worry, Carmen," he assured me. "The company is going to cover it."

It was afternoon, and Herb had just gotten home from work. The girls were at school, and we talked in the kitchen while I made their after-school snack.

"They're not going to pay for it," I scoffed, laying out Toll

House chocolate chip cookie dough on a baking sheet. "Why would they pay for it? It's our personal vehicle."

"No, don't worry. They'll cover it. I've already talked to my boss."

"Well, if I were you, I'd make sure," I snapped. I closed the oven, set the timer, and walked away.

Since the car was mine, I was the one who later received a notice from the LA Parking Violations Bureau; the tickets were up to fourteen hundred dollars. Herb and I were married by now, and I hit the roof.

"I don't know why you're being so irresponsible!" I exploded. "It's *my* name on the car. You said this was going to get taken care of."

Herb quieted, the way he usually did when he had to admit guilt or take criticism. It was one of my only complaints about him.

"Why is it so hard for you to tell me these things?" I continued. "You didn't tell me until way after you got the tickets, and you didn't tell me they hadn't been paid. Can you explain why that is so difficult for you?"

"I don't know."

"'I don't know.' It's always 'I don't know' with you, Herb."

He said nothing, his expression blank.

I took a deep breath. "Look," I said. "It's not a big deal. We can pay it. But I need you to tell me when these things happen. You can't keep hiding them. Can you do that?"

Herb nodded, unconvincingly.

"I won't blow up, okay? I'll appreciate you being honest."

"All right," he said.

"Good."

To me, the issue was addressed. He paid off the tickets and, as he promised, told me the next time he got one. He stuttered, hands shaking, as he showed me the piece of paper saying he owed forty-five dollars. Forty-five dollars—no big deal! But I could see how hard this was for him. It made me realize how low his self-esteem must be if he didn't feel comfortable telling his own wife about things like this.

"So we'll pay it," I said calmly. "Thank you for being honest."

Herb nodded but didn't look at me directly. No amount of understanding on my part, I saw, would relieve his discomfort. Whatever had happened in his life to make him this way, I would probably always need to be gentle with his emotions.

After that, life went on as it had: we worked hard, took care of the girls—Herb took them to school, made them meals, and watched them when I had my twelve-hour weekend shifts—and enjoyed our time together. We were newlyweds. Whatever small issues came up were dealt with quickly and easily.

It wasn't until just after September 11, 2001, that we had our first major blowout: I received the cable bill and saw that Herb had charged two porn movies. I was stricken—not because he was watching it but because he was hiding it from me.

"What is this, Herb?" I asked, showing him the bill. "Why wouldn't you tell me about this? If you want something different in our sex life, just ask."

Herb sat on the edge of our bed. He didn't respond.

"Just *talk* to me," I said.

"I think I have a problem."

"Problem?" I laughed. "Herb, renting a couple of porn movies hardly means you have a problem." (In hindsight, he may have also been visiting the triple-X theaters that were ubiquitous in LA.)

"I don't know," he said.

"You don't know. Well, why don't you go to therapy if you think you have a problem?"

"No, I'm not going to do that."

I could see Herb shutting down. My chest grew tight with frustration. Between Herb's reticence and my flair for the dramatic, it wasn't long before the argument escalated. Soon, I was crying and we were shouting at each other.

"Look, I just don't think I can be with you guys," he said, his dark eyes avoiding mine.

My heart dropped. "What are you talking about?"

Herb didn't answer.

"Herb, what are you *talking* about? We've been married six weeks. Now you're going to leave?" I yelled. "Are you fucking stupid?"

My language startled him—we never swore at each other—and he immediately backtracked. "No—of course not. I didn't mean it. Carmen—"

"I don't want to hear it," I said, leaving the room in tears.

I couldn't get his words out of my mind. The next day, when the kids were in school, we returned to the same fight. "So, are you going to leave then?" I asked coldly.

"No."

"If you don't want to be with us, maybe you *should* leave."

"Carmen, I didn't mean what I said."

"Well, I believe you did," I said, my voice rising. "So let's just end it, then. I don't want to fucking be with you anyway."

"I said I didn't mean it!" he yelled back.

I was standing in the doorway of our bedroom, and

fury radiated from us both. He stalked up to me and, for the first time in our relationship, screamed in my face. I was so shocked that I didn't even hear (nor do I remember) what he said; I only knew that he used the word *fuck*. For the first and only time, when I looked into his eyes, I was afraid of him. Even then, I didn't know why. He was yelling—we both were—but he wasn't being aggressive. He didn't threaten me and wasn't near hitting me; I never even considered that possibility.

"Don't you dare try to intimidate me like that," I said shakily.

He brushed past me and out the door.

That dark feeling lingered after the fight was over. Crying, I called Kess from the bathroom. "He doesn't want to be with me," I sniffed.

"Carmen, you're upset," she said. "You know that's not true."

"If I ever get killed, you can look at him."

My words startled us both. Where had *that* come from? I had no idea, and Kess didn't take me seriously. I didn't take myself seriously. Like Kess had said, I was just upset. It was a knee-jerk reaction out of hurt and anger. It wasn't long before we both forgot I'd said it at all.

CHAPTER 3

DISTANCE OF MILES AND SOULS

FOR THE NEXT FEW WEEKS, I DIDN'T WANT TO BE around Herb. I had thought we were happy. Didn't he feel the same? What was keeping him from being open with me? I had always thought of myself as understanding and nonjudgmental, yet my own husband didn't seem able to talk to me. Depressed and confused, I found myself wondering if I had made a mistake in marrying him. Just the thought tore me up.

Years back, when Herb and I were still just dating, he'd told me he was going to therapy every two weeks. Six months after showing me his dirty apartment, he said he was going to stop.

"Why?" I asked.

We were in the kitchen of my apartment in Culver City, and Herb was sitting on the counter. "I just don't think I need to go anymore," he said.

"I want you to continue going."

"Why?" he asked sharply. "Carmen, I was going because

my apartment was such a mess and I didn't know why I was like that. But if I'm going to live with you, I'm not going to be that way, so I don't need it."

Something didn't quite ring true. If he had been going for some time because of his apartment, why wasn't his carpet vacuumed? Why was his place still such a disaster? Some therapist, if that was the case.

"Herb—"

"We're friends, aren't we?" he interrupted. "We talk. Why do I need to see someone else?"

"Of course we talk," I said. "But I don't want to be your therapist."

Later, he wrote me a note—the only note he ever wrote me—saying that I was right, that he should continue trying to work out his issues in therapy. He didn't; he stopped going. After our blowout fight, I was more convinced than ever that he needed to see someone. If telling me about things like parking tickets and porn was so impossible, there were deeper issues at work that had nothing to do with me.

Eventually, things settled back into place. There was no more talk from Herb about leaving, and I let the subject drop. As fall turned to winter, we regained our easy comfort and intimacy.

We lit the fireplace as soon as the weather cooled. I had gotten used to the California winter, and while forty degrees was spring in Vermont, it chilled me now. Herb hadn't grown up with a fireplace, and the first time he tried to light it, I had to remind him to open the damper so smoke wouldn't fill the house. He struggled with the timber, trying to ignite a thick stack that didn't catch the flame; it wasn't unlike when he had tried to light my furnace years ago. Not wanting to bruise his ego, I let him try for a while before smiling and touching his shoulder.

"This is how I always did it," I said, reaching for some newspaper. I crumpled the thin paper and arranged it in the fireplace. Then I laid some little kindling on top. "If you pile it loosely, air can pass through from underneath and the fire will light better. See?"

Side by side, we watched the edges of the newspaper begin to blacken and curl before the wood crackled with heat.

"Yeah," Herb said sheepishly. "I get it."

We sat in front of the fireplace, shoulders touching, as warmth emanated. I sighed in contentment. "That feels so good."

From that point on, we lit the fire every winter Sunday before watching football, which Herb and I both loved. We also sometimes lit it at night during the week. It took Herb a few more attempts to get it right, but he eventually got the knack for arranging the newspaper and kindling just so. After that, lighting the fire was his job. His dark eyes were warm, his clean-shaven face open with satisfaction, each time he made the flames crawl over the wood. I thought that, as a man, he enjoyed being able to bring heat to his house full of girls.

∘ ∘ ∘

One night, sometime in the first year we were married, I shivered as the strangest feeling came over me in the shower. It was a malicious male energy, brief but powerful. As I got out and wrapped myself in a towel, I said to Herb, "I must have been a bad man in a past life."

Herb looked at me quizzically. "What do you mean?"

I shook my head and hung up my towel. "I just got this funny feeling in the shower—like of a man who treated women badly. It was the weirdest thing."

The feeling returned a couple of times, always brief and always when I was in the shower. I didn't know what to make of it, and I always forgot about it almost immediately afterward, once daily life resumed.

And it was so easy to get *consumed* with daily life. The routine was mind-numbing: twelve-hour shifts three days a week, during which Herb took the girls to school and picked them up; stagnating in traffic; getting home; eating dinner; helping with homework; going to bed.

Several times, I said to Herb, "I want something different."

"What do you mean?" he asked. "Something different than our life? Aren't you happy?"

I took his hand and scooted closer to him on the couch. "Of course I am. I'm fine. But I want something more. I don't want what I see everyone else having, because they don't seem happy."

I thought about my friends, their lives, and their relationships. More and more, it seemed we all followed the same path: build a career, buy a house, get married, have kids, raise a family. It was a mindless path, one ingrained in us from when we were children, and I knew so few people who were genuinely, deeply *happy* in it. I felt a pull in a direction I couldn't quite see. It was like a fierce craving without any sense of what my body actually *needed*. Without knowing, I didn't know what to reach for.

"What do you want us to do?" Herb asked.

"I don't know."

On the phone with Kess, I said, "Maybe I want to write a book. You're a good writer. Can you help me?"

"What kind of book?" Kess asked.

I sighed. The truth was that I didn't know. "I feel like I could help people be happy. I'm just not sure how."

Kess laughed. "I'm not going to help you write a book. It would end up being all about me!"

I let the subject drop.

° ° °

The girls' relationship with Herb was good when they were younger. I had told him early on, "I need you to help me raise these kids. I need you to discipline them when you need to if I'm not there," but Herb didn't know how to discipline. He was uncomfortable in that position—in retrospect I realize that children never respond well to being disciplined by someone new—so, rather than "tell" them what to do, Herb made it fun.

I asked that he and the girls keep the house picked up during the weekends. I didn't want to come home after a twelve-hour Saturday to the girls' toys and Herb's PlayStation equipment scattered all over the floor. So, in preparation for my arrival at eight o'clock, he'd tell the girls at seven, "Okay, girls, it's pick-up time before Mom comes home. We don't want Mom to be mad at us." The girls joined in the cleaning, and the house was tidy by the time I opened the door.

Once, I was relieved from work early and when I got home, the place was in shambles. I gaped, and Herb and the girls looked at me with big, busted eyes.

"Sorry, Carmen," he said. "We didn't know you were coming home, and we don't do anything until seven o'clock. I messed up," he added with a wry grin.

I shook my head, laughing. "Seven o'clock, huh? Very clever. Now, come on, let's all pick up."

There were times Herb's reluctance to discipline the girls frustrated me, but he did step in when they were giving me a particularly hard time. "You have a really good mom," he'd say to them during tantrums. "You need to stop treating her like that, because she is really good to you."

Liza, always a little rougher around the edges (like her mother), was never overly affectionate with Herb, but when she hit her preteen years, her attitude toward him worsened. She talked back and rolled her eyes, making it clear that she neither liked nor respected him. Of course, she was just as rude to Hannah and me, and it took me some time to stop being hurt by her cutting remarks. I had to remind myself of the teenager I had been—terrible!—and that it was just a phase. Herb wasn't able to shrug it off as easily.

"She doesn't like me," Herb said one night, his voice wounded.

"It's not personal," I assured him. "She doesn't like anyone right now. It's her age. Let her be the grump she is. She'll get over it."

Herb shook his head. "I don't think so."

"You know what?" I said, kissing his cheek. "It will all be worth it the day she gets married and you walk her down the aisle. You deserve that. If you put in the effort, you'll get those kinds of rewards."

Herb stayed quiet, and I knew he didn't feel the same way.

Stepparenting is the hardest job in the world. I wanted Herb to be closer to Liza, but I wasn't going to push either one to be someone they weren't. Whatever their relationship would be, I accepted it.

It wasn't long before Herb pulled away from the girls, especially Liza. He used to take them to McDonald's on weekends, or bring them to see me at work, or help them with school projects or with their softball team. He was their assistant coach, and I was the team mom. While he helped with practice, I organized and ran the candy sales and kept the scorebook. We enjoyed it, and the girls seemed to like having both of us involved. As a family, we went to the girls' games, cheering on the sidelines in the warm California sun. But now he seemed disconnected. He wasn't secure enough to brush off Liza's adolescent sharpness, and I couldn't help him because he didn't admit it.

"You don't feel comfortable around the girls anymore, do you?" I asked.

Herb's gaze remained fixed on the TV, where he was playing PlayStation. "I don't know."

"You get home from work and just do this until it's time for bed. You're not paying any attention to them, at least not when I'm around."

I watched Herb's thumbs flick over the controllers.

"Oh," I said. "So you're just not going to answer me."

He didn't respond.

"Well, then, I guess we aren't going to talk about it," I said, stalking off.

It seemed to be in Herb's nature to take things personally. I saw it even with the little things. Each night as we ate dinner, he waited for someone to thank him for cooking or to compliment the food. If I forgot, he eventually became quiet and pouty.

"You must not like dinner tonight," he said one evening, cutting into his chicken.

"What?"

"You must not like the food."

"Oh!" I shook my head. "No, Herb, it's delicious."

"Well, you didn't say anything."

"I'm sorry," I said. "I was distracted, but it's really good. Thank you for cooking."

He reminded me of a little girl during these times, turning up his nose and huffing because I hadn't given him what he wanted. There were days I soothed his hurt feelings and others when I told him what I needed to say even if he was pissy. I gave him the opportunity to break through those emotional barriers, but if Herb wasn't going to share his emotional life with me the way I did with him, I didn't think I could help him. And was it my *responsibility* to help him just because I was his wife? Did I want that kind of burden, that kind of dependence? Did I need to condemn myself to unhappiness just because he seemed unhappy?

"Our relationship isn't moving forward anymore," I said one day, almost in tears with frustration. "You're disconnected from the girls. You don't trust me—and I don't think it's just *me*. You don't trust anybody. Herb, I really wish you would go back to therapy."

"I've told you already," he said, shaking his head. "I don't want to go to therapy. I don't need it."

"Well, I'm moving forward with or without you. You know I'm here for you, and I've tried to make you happy, but it's obviously not helping." I took a breath and steadied my voice. "I love you and I want to be with you, but you're responsible for your own happiness. I need to find mine."

From then on, I took my focus off what I didn't like about our relationship and spent time immersing myself in what was good in my life. I concentrated on doing a good job at work, where I felt liked and appreciated and had a lot of friends, and I practiced letting go of the stress accumulated there on my drive home. Sometimes with the radio on, sometimes off, I used my commute to intentionally release any heaviness from my shift—a bureaucratic argument, a patient coding, a silly mistake. I didn't want to burden Herb or the girls with negativity. By the time I walked through the front door, I wanted to be fully present as a wife and mother. It was a skill I developed over time, compartmentalizing the aspects of my life that brought anxiety and enjoying those that gave me pleasure.

I didn't treat Herb any differently during this time. I still called him every day, kissed him when I got home, and asked how his day was. On the surface, nothing had changed. We talked about what married people usually talk about—what had happened at work, who had said what, the meal we would eat for dinner that night. Emotional conversations were rare, but I knew how much I loved him. I also knew he loved me. If Herb resented me for finding my own happiness, I didn't know it.

There was only one time I felt him push back. I had started a side business, CNH Legal Nurse Consulting, in 2003. Malpractice suits were common in California, and attorneys on both sides of the fence often needed the expertise of someone in the field. As a nurse, I could decipher cramped doctors' handwriting or the many abbreviations on patient charts, advising clients whether a case should be taken to court or settled. I also served as an expert witness when needed.

Herb supported me in my venture. He knew it would likely be six or eight months before I actually started making money, but he didn't mind being the breadwinner.

"There was a time in the late seventies when I did the same thing," he said. "I took my retirement and didn't work for six months. I just did what I wanted to do. I know this is important to you, Carmen, so you can do that."

I felt lucky to be married to someone who would sup- port me financially and emotionally; he believed in me.

In 2004, I had just finished a big case. A check came in for $2,400—the largest single check I had made with my business. Herb and I were doing well financially; debt was paid off, and the extra money meant we could live quite comfortably. After that check arrived, though, Herb couldn't share in my excitement.

"You know," he said, "I want a new car."

"What's wrong with what you have?" I asked.

"I don't want to drive that company truck anymore. I don't want to carry commodes and walkers, and if I have my own car, they can get someone else to do that stuff."

"Herb, it's medical equipment," I said. "It's your job. There's nothing wrong with that."

"Well, you got a new car two years ago." His voice was defiant, stubborn as a child's. "It's my turn."

I prickled. "It always seems, Herb, like when something really good is going on in my life, you have to steal my limelight."

Herb didn't respond.

I exhaled, staring at him. "Fine. You don't have a bal- ance on your credit card. Go put a thousand dollars down and I'll figure out the rest."

Another car payment would stilt whatever breathing room we were currently enjoying, but I didn't want to fight. So Herb bought a black Saturn Ion, and he was thrilled. He loved everything about it: the CD player, the gas mileage, and the fact that it wasn't a bulky work truck. He beamed as he took the girls and me for a drive.

"Herb, the steering wheel is so small," I said, laughing at how oversized his hands looked wrapped around it.

He laughed, too. "You'll get used to it if you drive it."

I was glad to have contributed to these moments of happiness, not realizing that it wasn't real; how could it be, with a material thing as the cause? And if happiness isn't real, it can't last.

∘ ∘ ∘

In June of 2005, I was painting the living room when Herb walked in.

"Yeah," he said, holding the phone to his ear. "Two girls. Liza's in seventh grade. Hannah's in fifth. They're great kids."

Liza twisted around on the couch. "Who's Herb talking to?"

"I don't know," I said curiously.

His voice was friendly and animated, as if he were catching up with an old friend. He chatted for a few more minutes before hanging up.

"I just called my sister," he said. "I'm going to call my mother."

"My god," I said, shocked. He hadn't talked to his mother in fifteen years or seen anybody in his family for thirty.

When he reached his mother, he asked me, "Do you want to say hello?"

I was flabbergasted as I accepted the phone. I knew precious little about his family and had no idea what to say. "Hello," I said. "This is Carmen."

"Hello, Carmen." His mother's voice was soft. She was seventy-four at the time. "So, you're Herb's wife?"

"Yes, we were married four years ago." I walked around the living room, making nervous small talk. The conversation was general and bare. I told her we had two girls, but they were from my previous marriage. I said we were very happy. I knew she was an LPN, so I told her I was a nurse at UCLA. I didn't know what else to say. Neither did she. Less than a minute later, I passed the phone back to Herb, and he spoke with his mother briefly before hanging up.

"What made you call them?" I asked.

Herb shrugged. "I don't know."

"Did something prompt this? Is anything going on?"

"No," Herb said, as simply as if I'd asked whether he'd eaten a sandwich for lunch.

After that, though he wasn't upset, he stopped answering my questions. I racked my brain, trying to figure out why he would make those calls *now*, but I couldn't think of a reason. Some time later, he told me it was because he'd just turned fifty. He was emotional about that milestone, thinking he was entering the dim years of his life. To my knowledge, he never called them again. The only thing I knew was that he and his sister emailed occasionally.

One day, I asked him whether he'd heard from her recently.

"No," he said sullenly. "And I don't think I'm going to email her anymore."

"Why not?"

"She doesn't write me personal letters. She just sends these email forwards—jokes and stuff. Obviously, she doesn't really want to talk to me."

That was it. The communication with his family ended as abruptly as it had started.

There was a part of Herb that I did not know—that he would not reveal. I finally accepted that I had to let it go. It wasn't my responsibility to search that part out, to heal whatever pain he refused to share. Over time, though, the more at peace I became with myself, the more miserable Herb grew. I wasn't aware of how much my control over my own life weighed on Herb—how he struggled against it. The only "power" I knew I possessed was as a mother.

In 2006, Liza was in the eighth grade and still acting out. She lied about little things, just to see if she could get away with it, and spent most of her time at friends' houses. I had raised my kids to be independent, to live for themselves instead of me or anyone else, but Liza was taking that a little too much to heart. She spit in the face of any kind of parental rules or demands and continued to treat everyone in the family disrespectfully.

Once, she came home from school and said, "Herb dropped me off today, and my friends saw him."

"So?" I asked.

"They said, 'Oh, we didn't know your father was black.'" Her voice dripped with condescension. "I was like, 'No, no, that's my stepfather. I'm white.'"

Liza and Hannah were two of the only white kids at their city school. They hung out mostly with Latinos, who, in turn, mostly stayed away from the black kids. Liza was afraid her friends would shun her if they thought she was half-black.

"Liza, honey," I said, "it's fine if you're a follower as long as you know what you're following. But I'd rather you lead your own life."

Liza huffed and walked away.

Some of her behavior was inevitable, and I was loose on disciplining her. When her grades dropped to Cs and Ds, however, I had to step in.

"We are not living this way," I said, glaring right back at her. "No phone. No TV. No computer. You're doing nothing but going to school and coming home."

"Mom!" she said. "You can't just take everything away—"

"Liza," I interrupted, "you are treating everybody in this family like shit. It's your turn. You're grounded until you're sick of acting that way. Because, let me tell you, I already am."

Between struggling with Liza and recognizing that I couldn't make Herb happy no matter how supportive I was, my frustration built. I was tired of being in the city, tired of the routine, tired of feeling as though I was running in circles. Maybe, after ten years in LA, it was time to return to Vermont. The small schools would be better for the girls, and maybe the change was what we needed as a family. The more I thought about it, the more going home seemed like a good idea.

When I decided I wanted to move back, I thought carefully about what to tell Herb. I knew how much I loved him, but I also knew I couldn't help him. The best thing I could do for him—for us both—was to let him know that I valued our individual joy more than staying together simply because we had committed.

"You didn't sign up to move to Vermont," I said, "and I see now that there's always been a part of you that hasn't been happy with us. We can sell the house and split the money. You can do your own thing."

I waited, watching him. He was my husband; I didn't want to get divorced. But I knew things were harder for him than me in our family. Teenagers are difficult, and they weren't his kids. I just wanted to give him the opportunity to make a decision for his own happiness. For the few moments before he responded, I imagined him saying, "Carmen, we're *married.* I'm in love with you. Of course I'll go."

What he said was, "I need to think about it."

His response floored me. It seemed to confirm everything I'd felt about things not being right with us, even though on the surface everything was fine. There was no fighting or animosity. We still talked, kissed, and made love. Yet he needed to think about whether to move with us. My first hurt, prideful response was to say, "You know what? Forget it. I don't want you to go anymore." But I told him to take his time and let me know.

The next day, Herb arrived at his answer. "I'm going to Vermont," he said.

I let my breath out in a long exhalation of relief and hope. While I was still hurt, I couldn't help feeling optimistic. We were going to make a lot of money on the house. He would have a hundred thousand dollars in his pocket if he chose to leave us, but he opted to stay. I took that as a sign of his commitment, an indication that he wanted to try harder at our marriage. Vermont would be a new start.

experienced the city life and the country life. You'll have a better understanding of both, so when you're older, you can make these decisions for yourself."

We put the house on the market, and just as I'd figured, we made a killing. We paid off all our debt and had plenty left over to buy a house in Thetford, Vermont, where we would be moving. Thetford was about fifteen miles from Lebanon, New Hampshire, where I used to work at Mary Hitchcock Memorial Hospital. Now called Dartmouth-Hitchcock Medical Center, the hospital needed nurses, and I easily found a job there.

We made two trips to Vermont before moving. The first was during the girls' April vacation from school, when we went for three or four days. Liza and Hannah didn't particularly like it. The weather was cold, with a constant sideways rain falling that cast a gloom over Thetford. I assured them it wouldn't always be that way.

The next month, Herb and I went back by ourselves. The few days we spent there were almost like vacation. We looked at houses during the day and spent time with my family and friends at night. The first night, we stayed at my dad's place. The next, we stayed at my brother's, and we spent the last two nights with my longtime friends Kathie and Bill. They had owned the convenience store I worked at throughout and after high school, and Kathie and I had gone to LPN and RN school together. Later, we'd found jobs at Hitchcock. She was more than twenty years older than I was, and our relationship was a strange but familiar cross between friends and a mother/daughter dynamic. She had retired from nursing five years earlier because she'd had open-heart surgery, and she and Bill had sold their three convenience stores long ago. Bill had always been a father figure to me—warm and caring but careful to keep a certain distance. It was nice to spend time with them again.

The night we stayed at my brother's, I saw Herb get drunk for the first time. It was Saturday night, and we were sitting in the dining room adjoining the kitchen. My brother, Donny; his wife, Jeanie; and Herb and I were drinking beer and playing cards. Matt, my nephew, had gone to bed, and the four of us stayed up till one in the morning, talking and laughing. Herb was the only one who got drunk. He was silly, his words slurring, telling jokes that made no sense and looking at me with glazed, loving eyes. It was the first time I'd seen him like this, and I laughed as much as Donny and Jeanie did. As much fun as we'd been having, he must have been uncomfortable, I realized. Visiting my family and moving to a new place was more stressful on him than anyone. Letting loose that night must have been a relief.

The next day, after looking at several homes, we found one we both fell in love with: it was white clapboard, brand new, without any of the old-house problems that plagued us with our 1940s Hawthorne home. It was set on a couple of acres, with rows of towering, fragrant pines bordering the yards. Best of all, it was close to Liza and Hannah's schools. In complete agreement, Herb and I made an offer. We were both excited for the move and eager for something new.

Herb, however, was going to struggle to find work. He wasn't from the Upper Valley; he couldn't pick up the phone and secure a job the way I had. He also wasn't highly educated, and—with a population of less than three thousand—there weren't many options in Thetford anyway; certainly there wasn't anything that would pay what he had earned in California. There, he had willingly taken on the role of breadwinner for eight or nine months while I started my consulting business. I decided to extend the same gift.

"Don't worry about finding a job right away," I said. "We've got plenty of money. Just stay home for a while and get to know the town."

At first he was hesitant. I could understand that. Rarely is a man comfortable letting his wife support the family. But he eventually agreed, and on June 26, we packed our bags. As I made plane reservations, I thought of Herb's short-lived communication with his mother and sister the year before.

"Do you want to stop by Camden and see your family?" I asked.

"No," Herb said.

"Are you sure? Why not?"

"I just don't need to see them."

"Well ... all right."

So we made the flight without the detour.

To my surprise and delight, our first five or six weeks in Vermont were the best of our marriage. I didn't have to start work until August, and away from the daily routine in which we'd been so ingrained, Herb and I got to spend quality time together. Our bank accounts were padded with the money from our house sale, so we were freer than we'd ever been to simply be with each other and our family. The money also gave us certain liberties. We had a truck coming with some of our furniture and boxes from California, but we were going to buy a lot of new things. As a family, we shopped for beds, nightstands, and dressers for the kids. We picked out towels, blankets, games—all those things, large and small, that make a house one's own.

For six weeks, we didn't set our alarm clock and we didn't make plans. We did what we wanted to do. During the hottest time of the afternoons, we took the kids to the lake to swim. They donned bathing suits and launched, shrieking, into the cool, clear water. Herb and I swam, too. I wrapped my legs around him, and he held me close. We were buoyant, weightless. Afterwards, we took the girls to get ice cream. They liked the soft serve chocolate and vanilla swirl. I always got a fudge sundae. Herb switched his order each time, but he preferred the hard scoop ice cream, especially Ben and Jerry's Cherry Garcia.

I felt more connected to Herb than I had in years, and it seemed the feeling was mutual: we were having sex all the time, the way we used to when we were first married. Any chance we got, we were together in bed, and I could tell from a look in his eye or the pressure of his hand what he was thinking about if we were out with friends. Those weeks were like a second honeymoon, and I couldn't get enough.

Besides reconnecting with Herb and spending time with the girls, I used my free weeks to re-establish relationships with family and friends. I saw my dad, brother, and sister-in-law regularly, as well as Kathie and Bill. I also called up Linda, an elementary school friend. I'd last seen her in 1998, when the girls and I had visited Vermont. I'd gone to her home to see her and Jennifer, her girlfriend at the time. I wasn't sure if this was the right number, but I took a stab and left her a message. She called back a few days later, and she and her son came to our house for dinner not long after. Herb and I were in the kitchen, chatting as he cooked spaghetti, when the doorbell rang.

I rushed to the front door and flung it open. "Hi!" I exclaimed, laughing.

"Carmen!" Linda said, just as excitedly. We hugged each other tightly. "It's been way too long. God, something smells good!"

Linda was around my height, five-three, and stocky, with red hair, blue eyes, and a smattering of freckles across her nose and cheeks. Her son, Josh, was eleven, Hannah's age. He was a good-looking boy, half-black with big dark eyes and soft curls. Jennifer had left some time after Josh was born.

"Come on in," I said. "Meet Herb and the girls. The spaghetti is just about ready."

We trooped into the kitchen, where I made introductions and called out to the girls to come eat. We had a great time over the casual meal, laughing and catching up. I told Linda how Herb and I had met at UCLA, and she bragged about what an exceptional athlete Josh was, though he was only in sixth grade. He accepted her praise matter-of-factly, as though he was used to hearing it and agreed wholeheartedly.

Later, when the kids were in the living room watching TV, the adults relaxed with a few drinks. Linda drank quickly, her fair skin flushing with the alcohol.

"I'm so glad you're back," she said. She hopped off her chair and came to mine, dropping into my lap. She threw an arm over my shoulder and smiled as the three of us continued talking.

Liza, coming into the kitchen for a glass of water, got a little jealous glint in her eye when she saw Linda on my lap. She set her glass on the counter and squirmed on top of me beside Linda. I nudged Linda off with my thigh. "Kids," I said, bouncing Liza. "The minute you're not paying attention to them, they want you."

Linda laughed, too. "Josh is exactly the same."

I loved being back in the Upper Valley. It felt like coming home. For me, it wasn't a big adjustment being back in small-town life. I loved going to the outdoor shopping mall in New Hampshire, and it took only ten minutes on the interstate to get anywhere; I was so used to LA traffic that I never complained about a traffic jam again.

In August 2006, I returned to work at Hitchcock. The hospital had largely remained the same. It was a new building in 1991, and it was as clean and freshly painted in 2006 as it was back then. While there weren't as many familiar faces, some of the nurses I'd worked with were still there. Right away, I ran into Thomas, a nursing assistant at the hospital I'd known since I was twenty. He was a gentle soul. Short—five feet, four inches—stocky, and strong. By the time I left for LA, he was married with a son. When I returned, he was working on Four West, the inpatient unit where I used to work, doing post-op care for patients who'd undergone vascular and cardiothoracic surgeries. I recognized him instantly, and Thomas broke into a huge smile when he saw me.

"Hey!" he greeted me. "It's been a long time. How are you?"

"Ten years," I said, smiling. "And doing great, just moved back here with my husband and kids."

"Bet it's a big adjustment from LA, huh?" he asked.

"Not as much as you'd think. I love being back." I smiled. "What about you? Are you still married? How's your son?"

Thomas made a face and shrugged. "Divorced. Sixteen years. Josh is twenty. Your daughters would be younger than that, but you know how teenagers are."

I laughed. "Boy, do I. Anyway, I've got to get back to work. I'm sure I'll be seeing you around."

My workdays were busy. I either had a patient assignment, like the other nurses, or I was a "resource nurse," watching over the floor and doing bed control with patients coming out of surgery. If I wasn't performing either of those two duties, I was working with recent nurse graduates, getting them to a place where they could take their own assignments. We also did physical care, such as beds and baths, and administered all medications and drips. In between shifts, I called home as I always had. When the girls were little, I felt the need to check up on them often. Now it was a habit; even though the girls didn't wait around for those calls anymore, it was still a chance to talk to Herb throughout the day.

The girls started school the same month I returned to work. Liza was very social; she was a freshman and wanted to meet people, so she joined JV soccer. She'd never played any school sports before except for the years she'd done organized Little League softball. Hannah, who was in the seventh grade, ran junior high cross-country track. Both of them made friends quickly and adjusted wonderfully to the move.

As the pace of life picked up, I also began spending more time with my dad. My parents had divorced when I was eleven, and our family was never particularly tight knit. For a long time, it ate at me how distant we all were from one another, and I tried to bind us together with phone calls and attempts at arranging visits. It took me a long time to realize that I couldn't be the family's linchpin; the unit—if it could be called one—just didn't function that way. Instead, I focused on maintaining my relationship with individual family members rather than trying to mend everyone else's fences.

Just before I started work, Dad's wife left him. I knew he was distraught and went over to his house at least four times a week to listen to him; I, too, knew the misery of a disintegrated marriage, and I wanted to support him. Dad's wife was twenty years younger than he was, and she left less than a year after they were married.

"Dad, her leaving is not something you could control," I told him. "It was her choice, and she's the one who should feel bad for it, not you."

Dad's handsome face was wan with pain. He looked at me as though he wanted to believe me but couldn't. I didn't think he'd ever been hurt like this, and expressing his emotion was uncharacteristic. He was a man who took care of his business, never leaning on others for support, so confiding in me was beyond unusual.

Dad sighed. "I don't know what I was thinking."

After a few weeks of this, Herb's cheerful demeanor began changing. He no longer sounded happy to hear from me when I called from work. There were long, silent pauses in which I heard the telltale crashing and burning noises from his PlayStation game. When I came home after one of these calls, I said, "You act like you don't even want to talk to me."

Herb didn't miss a beat. "I don't. You don't have to call anymore."

My chest stung with heat. I didn't say anything. I just told the girls to text me if they needed anything and stopped calling home.

On one of my days off, Herb and I were smoking in the garage when he said moodily, "Are you going over to your dad's today? You've been over there all the time lately."

"He was there for me when I divorced," I reminded Herb. "I was over there all the time, crying on his shoulder. I'm not going to make excuses and not go."

"It's either him or you're on the phone with Linda. What's going on with her, anyway, sitting on your lap like that?"

"Herb, please. Don't tell me you're jealous."

Herb stared at me, blowing a stream of smoke.

"That's ridiculous. Okay, so she's a little inappropriate now and again, but it's just from us knowing each other for so long."

"Are you sure about that?"

"Herb! Besides, no matter what her intentions are, if she even has any, I'm not gay. You have no reason to be upset or jealous. Okay?"

Herb shrugged, and we smoked the rest of our cigarettes in silence.

"You're just never around anymore," he said.

"Are you kidding me?" I said. "You're the one who told me to stop calling you. We've always talked every day, no matter who is working. You don't even want me anymore."

I lit another cigarette to distract myself from tears. I wanted Herb to tell me I was wrong, but he simply slipped another cigarette from his pack as well.

"You're just like the girls," I said quietly. "You want me around in *case* you need me for something, but when I'm here, all you do is play those stupid video games. You don't even care."

I realize now that Herb did care; he just didn't have the maturity or awareness to express how he was feeling. At the time, I was just hurt. I didn't see that we'd been drifting apart for months, possibly years, and moving to Vermont only prolonged the inevitable.

After another long silence, Herb said, "I feel like you don't really care about our marriage anymore."

"That's not true at all, Herb. You *know* that's not true. Look," I said, "why don't you tell me what it is you want?"

"I don't know."

"Well, I don't read minds. If you don't tell me, I won't know how to give it to you."

I don't read minds. That was a line I'd said often over the years, but it didn't help. Herb seemed incapable of telling me what he needed.

Herb spiraled downward soon after that. He was home all day, and within a few months he had gained twenty pounds and been diagnosed with diabetes. He didn't complain about his life—Herb was never a complainer—but his unhappiness was palpable. Even on the days he was more upbeat, laughing at jokes and being playful, his cheer seemed artificial; there was no true joy in his eyes. It hurt to see him that way and know there was nothing I could do about it.

° ° °

Shortly after Hannah's twelfth birthday, she had what I now call a premonition.

It was a clear evening in October, and I was getting ready to leave for the night shift at the hospital. When I went to Hannah's room to say goodbye, I could hear her crying through the door. I let myself in to see her sitting on the floor beside her bed, weeping so hard her face was soaked. Immediately, I shifted into mother mode: "What's wrong, honey? What happened?"

"Something really, really bad is going to happen to you."

"What do you mean?" I asked, instantly unnerved. "What is going to happen?"

Hannah kept crying. I pressed to see if she would tell me more, but she could not. She only knew that something bad was on its way.

I drove to work cautiously that night, calling Hannah when I got there to assure her that I was okay. She was still crying, even when I called again at bedtime. I knew that Herb, who was home with the girls that night, was annoyed with her crying, but I didn't care—her feelings were strong and powerful, and I took them seriously. Hannah had always had a special energy about her. When she was ten months old and lying on my chest, I had looked into her old-soul eyes and asked, "What do you know that I don't?"

A few months later, in January, everything came to a head. I arrived home from work one night, and Herb said, "I've got to talk to you."

"Okay …," I said cautiously.

The kids were busy watching TV and doing homework, and I followed Herb into our bedroom. He handed me the television bill. The first page listed a hundred dollars of porn charges.

"I think I have a problem with watching this," he said.

In an instant, I knew that he had been watching much more than the bill let on; he must have been paying with his credit card. There was no doubt in my mind that he'd slipped up this time and was only telling me because

I would find out anyway. All the old anger built in my chest. We'd been married for almost six years, and it was the same old shit. The same little lies, the same keeping of secrets.

"*This* isn't the problem," I said, shaking the paper in the air. "It's a symptom. And I don't want to talk about it right now."

"Carmen—"

"No," I said. "I need to keep quiet, because I am not going to be nice right now."

I left the room and went down to the cellar. It was a small, dim space with a few boxes and some old gallons of paint. I grabbed the nylon folding chair that we used for the girls' sports games and unfolded it in the middle of the room. I swiped one of the packs of cigarettes and the ashtray and settled into the chair. I was just so tired of everything. The kicker was that the last few weeks had been *better.* Herb and I had gone on a diet, and he'd thrown himself into it, losing fifteen pounds in three weeks. We still had a little extra money in the bank, so I decided to make a living will. I named Kathie my health proxy and specified that the girls should live with Herb if anything happened to me—that was, if all three of them wanted it that way. Doing these things together and distancing myself slightly from Linda had seemed to make a positive difference. I thought there was a chance—more than a chance—of Herb and I getting back on track. All marriages had their hiccups. But now there was this. Again.

After the kids went to bed, I walked back into our bedroom. "Herb," I said, sighing. "I feel like I'm saying the same thing over and over again. You're not a sex addict.

This is a symptom of something else, but if you're not willing to talk to me about it, then go to therapy. Do *something*, because I don't want you lying to me anymore." My voice cracked. "I can't take it."

A few days later, I went over to Kathie's house. "Why can't he get through this?" I asked her, crying. "Why do we have this—this *block* in our relationship?"

I was sitting on her living room couch, and she sat on a chair across from me. Kathie was an opinionated woman, and I half-expected her to tell me to just leave, that she and Bill had never liked Herb anyway. She'd never expressed that to me, but lately they had been canceling dinner and movie plans with excuses I could see right through. Now, though, Kathie said, "He's probably having a hard time, moving across country, not having any friends and not working."

"I understand that," I said. "I really do. And if porn was the actual problem, then fine. But it's not—it's the lying and keeping secrets, and that was there long before we moved. I just can't deal with it."

When I returned home, I was emotionally exhausted. Herb was waiting for me.

"Is it okay if I go talk to your brother?" he asked.

I sighed. I didn't like Herb talking to members of my family after we fought. He had done that early on in our marriage, confiding in Kess about one of our arguments, and I told him that he had his own family; if he chose not to use them as support, that was fine, but I didn't want him splitting my family's loyalty. It wasn't a mature reaction, I knew, but it was how I felt. In Vermont, though, Kathie was right: Herb was isolated. He had no one else.

"If what you need is to talk to a guy, then fine," I said.

"Go talk to my brother if he's willing to listen to you."

Herb went over to my brother's house, and when he came back, he was in high spirits.

"Well, how did it go?" I said.

"It was good . . . but I asked that everything I said be held in confidence."

My annoyance flared. "So you're asking my brother not to say anything to me, and you're not going to tell me anything, either. That doesn't help our relationship, Herb."

"Look, I made an appointment for therapy," he said. "Carmen, I don't want to lie anymore. I'm going to take care of whatever this is. It's going to end."

I stared at him for a moment. His face was creased with anxiety. I could tell how much he truly wanted this to stop; I just didn't know how capable he was of changing.

"You go to therapy," I said, "and as soon as that therapist tells you we need marriage counseling, I'll go. I want happiness in my life, Herb."

"Me too," he said.

The tentative peace, with whatever hope for repair it brought, didn't last long. A week or two later, I couldn't find the cable bill when I went to pay it. When I asked Herb what happened to it, he said he'd taken care of it.

"Well, you didn't write a check," I said. "Where'd you get the money?"

"I went to the bank and took money from the savings account," he said. "I made out a money order."

"A money order?" I repeated, processing. "Why would you do that? I already knew about the bill. That makes no sense."

Herb didn't answer, and I was sick of trying to play a game when I didn't know the rules.

"We just had this big talk about keeping secrets, and then you go and do the same thing," I exploded. "How could you?"

"I don't know," he said. "I just can't stop lying, I guess."

"You know what? Forget it—I'm done."

"Carmen, I am so, so sorry," he said.

"Now you're all apologetic? It's too much, Herb. I can't do it anymore."

For the next few days, the air in our home was heavy with the weight of things unsaid. The happiness I'd managed to cultivate in myself in California, despite the low points in our marriage, was gone. Herb simply must not have the capacity to love me the way I once thought he did. The realization was heartbreaking.

A few days later, I came to him, crying. "I'm miserable, Herb," I said. "Just miserable."

Herb's face was pained; he hated seeing me cry. "Carmen, I can't hurt you anymore … I think we need to dissolve our marriage."

My heart dropped. "Are you saying you want to get divorced?"

"Yes."

I took a deep, shuddering breath. "Fine. Well, then, it's over, and I'm going to hold you to it this time. It may not have anything to do with me, but being with us is clearly not making you happy."

Herb lowered his head. He didn't respond.

"You'll have to find a job." I tried to keep my voice steady. "And an apartment. By next month, I want you gone."

I held Herb—and myself—to the decision and told the kids that night. Hannah called asking if she could spend the night at a friend's place, and I said no, asking her to come home instead.

"Am I in trouble?" she asked.

"No. I just need to talk to you and Liza together."

With Liza sitting on the computer chair and Hannah on the couch, I said, "Herb and I are breaking up. I can't do it anymore and neither can he."

The room was silent, and I burst into tears.

"Sorry," Hannah said.

"Well, that doesn't surprise me," Liza said. "You guys have been fighting a lot lately."

"Are you guys going to be okay with this?" I asked. I knew, of course, that it had been a long time since the girls had felt connected to Herb, but he had been in their lives for eight years at that point. He was the only father figure they knew.

"We'll be fine, Mom," Liza said. In a less certain voice, she asked, "Will you be okay?"

I took a deep breath and tried to get my tears under control. All I saw before me was heartbreak, a crumbling life. Forcing a smile, I said, "I'll get through it."

I took the girls to get pizza for dinner, and as we drove home in winter's early darkness, I remembered Hannah's premonition from months earlier. "Hey," I said to her, glancing in the rearview mirror. "Remember when you got upset that something bad was going to happen to me? Maybe this was it."

"Yeah," Hannah said, shrugging. "Maybe."

We drove the rest of the way home intermittently singing to the radio and sitting in comfortable silence. I loved our dynamic when it was the three of us. We were a whole unit. Maybe, I thought sadly, my relationship with Herb had taken away from them more than it had given.

° ° °

The next three and a half weeks passed at a painful crawl. Herb didn't have a job, so he couldn't just leave. He slept on the couch while he looked for an apartment and applied for work. Meanwhile, wanting to nip small-town rumors in the bud, I told my supervisors and co-workers that my husband was leaving me. I barely managed to say the words without crying.

One day, I was cleaning the kitchen table of its habitual clutter when I saw a thin sheaf of papers with Herb's name on them. Offhandedly, and with the familiarity of a wife, I flipped through them. It was a job application for JCPenney as well as a background check. The first page showed zero convictions, zero arrests. No surprises there. I collected the papers into a neat pile and set it aside for Herb. I hoped the job would come through quickly—I wanted him gone already. His blankets and pillows on the couch were a bitter reminder that I couldn't hold our marriage together. Worse, I couldn't figure out *why*. I was a nurse; I was used to identifying symptoms and using them to decode the underlying problem. But Herb was a mystery to me. Even now, after almost a decade of being together, he *confused* me.

There was no one I wanted to talk to about what was happening. Friends called, but I made up excuses to get off the phone. I was hurt, angry, and humiliated. I didn't want their concern. I didn't want to be coddled. I didn't want their opinions. I just wanted to be left alone. I hadn't gotten married a second time to get divorced, and yet here I was. The sense of failure and disappointment was crushing.

By the time Herb was supposed to move out, he didn't want to go.

"I'll work it out in therapy," he said. "Please. I promise."

"I'm tired of you saying that," I replied. "If you want us to be together, then you'll just have to leave and work on yourself alone. I'm not doing this any other way."

On a Sunday in February, I was at work and Hannah was at a friend's house. Liza and Herb were the only ones at home. I called Liza around five o'clock that evening to check in.

"Hey, honey," I said. "How's everything going?"

"Herb is gone."

"What? Where did he go?"

"He went to his apartment," she said. "He moved out."

I blinked. My chest felt bruised when I breathed in. "But—he wasn't supposed to go until Wednesday."

"Yeah, but Mom, he left." Liza paused. "I don't think he's coming back."

CHAPTER 5

LOST

AFTER HERB AND I SEPARATED, THE DAY-TO-DAY routine immediately changed. Liza and Hannah were only fourteen and twelve, so they couldn't drive themselves anywhere. A school bus passed through each morning, but it arrived in our area when it was still dark and left students at school an hour before the bell rang. Naturally, the girls objected to that option. Then I thought of Michelle, a friend of mine from high school. She lived in Lyme, New Hampshire, and her daughter was Liza's age. I asked if she could pick up and drop off the girls on days I worked; I tried to pick up an extra weekend shift so the favor would only encompass two days per week.

The days I didn't work were tough. I was alone in the house Herb and I had bought together, where we had enjoyed each other so much only six months ago. How could things have deteriorated so quickly? How could we have gone from two people so in love to … this?

I wandered around the house looking at family photos. I examined our faces, looking for proof we'd been happy, as well as evidence of when that started to sour. Every so often, I caught my reflection in the sun-and-moon mirror I had admired in a shop window, and which Herb had surprised me with later. He was always buying me little gifts. In the mirror, my eyes were bleak. I was thirty-eight years old and getting divorced for the second time. I had never felt so lost.

When the girls were home, I started asking questions about their relationship with Herb. There was so much about him that I didn't know and wanted to understand.

"What did Herb do when I went to work?" I asked. It was shortly after he moved out, and we were sitting in the living room. "Did he talk to you? Spend time with you?"

Hannah, always the more cautious and private of the two, listened but didn't answer. Liza stepped in.

"After he fixed dinner, he just went into the bedroom and closed the door," she said.

"Really?"

"Yeah." She rolled her eyes. "He always did that, especially if you worked the night shift. As soon as you left, he would go into the kitchen, tell us when dinner was ready, and that was it."

Hannah added, "We tried not to bother him unless we really needed something."

A thick cord of anger and sadness rose to my throat. How could he have been *so* disconnected from them? I knew it had been building up to this, and yes, he was still taking care of their physical needs, but I hated to think of the girls "trying not to bother him." I also ached at how obviously miserable Herb had been. What did he do when he went into the room by himself? Was that one of the many times of day he watched porn? Or did he just go quietly to sleep, alone with the emotions he wouldn't—or couldn't—share?

"Well, how do you feel about him leaving?" I asked them.

"It's fine with me," Liza said. "I never really liked him anyway. Sorry."

Despite knowing that Liza and Herb were never close, her matter-of-fact reaction surprised me a little. "Okay...," I said. "Hannah? What about you?"

"I agree with Liza," she said, the way she usually did when she wasn't comfortable sharing something.

Though she never said it, I suspected Herb leaving was harder on Hannah than she let on. She was only four when Herb and I started dating; whereas Liza had always butted heads with Herb, it was obvious that Hannah liked him. He returned her affections. Before he disengaged from them, he'd tried hard to please her. Hannah liked to sew, and Herb sat beside her on the living room floor, making sock puppets. Even though Hannah was angry, I knew she had to be hurting, too.

With Herb gone, I was miserable. The feelings I'd had for years, the desire for something more (whatever that was), grew into a savage ache in my chest: was this all I had to look forward to in life? Working hard, raising my kids? Would I always be alone? Additionally, Herb and I had bought a rental property in September, and I had leased it to Linda. All of her payments were coming in late, and none of her excuses rang true. I felt she wasn't being honest about who she was or the problems—particularly with alcohol—she was facing, and our interactions became increasingly uncomfortable. I decided the best, healthiest thing to do was to pull away from the friendship.

"Look," I said over the phone one day, "I'm going through a hard time right now. Please just pay me when you know you need to, and give me some space. I need to be alone."

Need to be alone. What a contradiction. As much as I wanted space from my friends' concern, actually being *alone* was the last thing I needed.

Despite our mutual suffering, Herb and I tried to remain friends. He had gotten a job in the men's department of the local JCPenney, and we talked on the phone at least once a week. I still felt connected to him and wanted to know he was doing well.

On April 10, Herb came over so we could file our papers together. He'd lost more weight and looked handsome but somewhat sad in my favorite purple shirt. He still wore his wedding ring. I sensed this was his last-ditch effort to change my mind, even if he didn't ask me directly.

We drove my car about thirty minutes north to the courthouse in Chelsea. I bawled the whole way up. As much as I knew this was the right decision, I was mourning the loss of what we'd had—the love I'd thought we would grow into.

Herb reached for my hand. "Carmen, I'm so sorry for everything. The way it all happened—I didn't mean—"

"I know. I'm sorry, too." I blinked hard, trying to stop the tears. "But we'll be okay apart. We'll learn from this and move on."

"You think so?"

"Yeah," I said, trying to convince myself as much as him. "I do."

"You know I still love you?"

I nodded, swallowing. "I love you, too, as a person. I probably always will. But I think the best we can do now is be friends."

It cost seventy-five dollars to file for divorce, and we had no debt except the mortgages on our house and the rental property. Both were in my name, and Herb willingly signed over the deed to both properties. In return, he kept ten thousand dollars in cash and a new truck. We had no children's visitation to work out, since neither he nor the girls had any interest in seeing one another; to Liza and Hannah, he had let me down, and they were angry about it. It must have seemed that he cared for me less than I cared for him; in retrospect, I don't believe he had the ability to care for me in the way I needed. In any case, all we had to do was wait three months for a total separation of six months, and our divorce would be finalized. As far as divorces went, ours seemed as though it would be easy.

After we filed, we drove back to my house. My eyes felt gritty from crying, and my head throbbed with a faint headache.

"Let me get you a cup of coffee," I said, walking into the kitchen.

"That'd be great." He followed me and sat at the bar. "Thanks."

I turned on my little Mr. Coffee machine and scooped a few spoonfuls of Maxwell House into the filter. Within a few minutes, the comforting scent we both loved filled the room. When it was ready, I poured him a cup and sat across from him.

"So, how're you liking work?" I asked, taking a sip of coffee.

Herb shrugged. "It's all right. Pays the rent. At least I don't have to be shuttling commodes around all day."

I smiled and shook my head. "Herb, it was a good job."

"Still."

After a few minutes, Herb looked pensive. "You know, my mother is disfigured."

"She is?" I asked, startled. "What do you mean?"

Herb stared into his coffee cup. "I don't know what happened. I was a little boy, but I think my father's wife threw something in her face—hot water, maybe—and it burned her."

I sat in silence for a moment, letting his words sink in. "Herb, we were together for a long time and friends before that—why wouldn't you have told me something like this?" I thought of the day he'd called his mom and sister and about all the questions I'd asked afterwards. That would have been a plenty good time to tell me.

"There's something else I want to tell you." The look on his face reminded me of when he'd shown me his apartment, tense and fearful. "I did use heroin. I was quite the druggie back in the seventies and eighties."

I stared at him. "*What?* Herb, I *asked* about that when we first met. Lying about little things is one thing, but you knew how important it was to me to ensure I wasn't at risk for HIV." My voice rose as I set my coffee cup down with a clatter. "I had the *girls*. Damn it, I would have made sure you were tested. How could you have put me in that position?"

"Carmen—"

"And why are you telling me about this *now*? Are you just doing it to hurt me?"

"I'm going to therapy," he said, "and I thought you would appreciate my honesty."

"Your *honesty*? You've lied about this the whole time! Jesus. I expected you to tell me the truth the first time I asked. What the hell does it matter now?"

For a few moments I just glared at him, breathing hard. His face was pained, his eyes begging me for something I couldn't give—forgiveness, maybe. Understanding. Hope.

"I need a cigarette," I said. I grabbed my pack and stalked past him toward the cellar. His footsteps followed behind me.

Once we were downstairs in the dim, cool room, Herb's mood changed. He was visibly bothered, his hand shaking as he lifted a cigarette to his lips. His breath, when he exhaled, was heavy and shuddering. I could tell he wanted to tell me things, share his truth—finally. Maybe he thought it would win me back or help us repair the relationship that was so much more damaged than I'd realized. But he was still too guarded to show real emotion. And, unlike when he had taken me to see his apartment, I was not open to the possibility.

"Carmen," he said, "there's another thing."

"No, Herb." I shook my head, tapping my cigarette above the ashtray. "I don't want to hear anymore, okay?"

"It's about my first wife. I got in trouble for hitting her. I—I slapped her. It was with an open hand, but still I—"

"What the *fuck*, Herb!" I burst into furious tears. "I've had it. I don't want to talk to you anymore. We're done—just get out."

"I just thought you should know," he said quietly.

"Yeah, now I know to never see you again, you damn asshole!" I shouted. "Just leave! Now!"

I stayed in the cellar as Herb left without another word. Shaking, I lit another cigarette. This was it, then. There was no longer anything I could do to convince myself to stay with him. He'd left me with nothing to ease the sting of betrayal and humiliation, nothing to stop the ragged pain of my heart breaking. He'd left me with nothing.

CHAPTER 6

HARBINGERS OF CHANGE

MY RUSH OF ANGER DISSIPATED AS QUICKLY AS IT had consumed me in the cellar, leaving a dull sadness in its place. I wished Herb and I had worked on the issues that came up once we moved to Vermont, but I reminded myself that he hadn't told me the truth from the beginning. It *killed* me that he didn't. The lies were so huge, the omissions so gaping, that it wouldn't have mattered if we'd addressed the surface issues. Our marriage suddenly felt like a farce from the start.

Though I was still so hurt, I thought it was in both our best interests if we remained friendly, if not actually friends. A couple of weeks after our last talk, he realized he'd forgotten to pay a fee and went to court to write a check. Afterwards, he stopped at the house to put a receipt in the mailbox. The kids were home, but I wasn't, and for reasons I couldn't fully express, I didn't like that.

"Don't be coming to the house when I don't know," I told him over the phone. "I don't want the kids to get upset by seeing you."

Shortly after we filed, a terrible windstorm hit the Upper Valley. The wind howled all night, but I couldn't tell the extent of the damage the next morning because it was still dark as I drove to work. The hospital was on top of a hill, and as I walked toward the entrance, I saw thousands of crows perched on the treetops nearby. All together, they shrieked and cackled. The noise was so overwhelming that it stopped me in my tracks. I grimaced at the shapes of so many birds, clutching branches that shook with the wind. The sight was eerie enough to make me hurry inside.

"Wasn't that strange?" another nurse asked as we stepped onto the elevator.

"Yeah, what's going on with those birds?" I replied, shuddering. "It feels like it's doomsday."

The kids were home from school that day, and they were woken by a great crack as a seventy-foot pine in our backyard snapped down the middle.

"We're scared," Liza said on the phone. "Can you come get us?"

"Of course, honey. I'll go by on my lunch break in an hour. Just stay inside the house, and call me if anything else happens."

The drive back home was sunny but very windy. I saw limb after limb strewn across sidewalks and streets, and the wind pushed my car out of its lane more than once.

The girls were on edge when I got home. "Look, Mom," Liza said, dragging me out back. "Look at the tree."

The backyard looked divided in half by a great big wind tunnel; branches were flattened where the wind had pushed through, and the enormous pine made a strange sight, cracked and horizontal on the ground.

"Let's go," I said.

I gave the girls some money at the hospital they could

use to grab pizza or chicken sandwiches. They hung out by the pizza place and gift shop while I worked for the next seven hours. In late afternoon, they came up to the front desk of my section. The floor had four desks, or "pods," as we called them, and my friend Thomas was working on the first. When my shift ended and I went to collect the girls, they were milling around Thomas's pod, chatting. I saw them before they saw me, and the open, friendly looks on their faces—especially Liza's—surprised me.

"All right, girls, time to go," I said. I smiled at Thomas. "Thanks for keeping them company."

He smiled back. "They're the ones who kept me entertained. See you guys later," he said to Liza and Hannah.

They waved back as we walked away, calling, "Bye, Thomas!"

In the car, Liza gave me a sly, sidelong look. "Is Thomas married?"

"No, he's not married," I said. "Why?"

"Well, he's real nice, Mom. Maybe you should see him."

I laughed. "Well, look at you, playing matchmaker."

They teased me about him the rest of the way home, and it stayed on my mind as I got ready for bed later. I had never thought of Thomas in that way before … but why not? He *was* nice, and I could use a distraction from everything going on with Herb.

As I drove to work later that week, I saw a falcon up in a tree. It was a kestrel, brown and white with a startling wingspan. The trees were still bare, their branches thin and drab. The falcon seemed to hold my stare as I drove past.

I worked with Thomas again that week, and we chatted after our shifts. He mentioned that his printer was broken, and I jumped in with, "You know, I actually have a printer we don't use at the house. You're welcome to have that if you need one."

"Really?" he asked, grinning broadly. "God, that'd be a lifesaver."

"Yeah, no problem."

"Do you want to bring it to work, or would you rather I go get it?"

I laughed. "Who wants to lug a heavy printer to work?" I wrote my phone number down on a scrap of paper. "Give me a call and let me know what your schedule is next week."

Thomas drove up the following week to pick up the printer. We ended up going out for breakfast, and he returned later that afternoon just to hang out. I made coffee, and we retreated to the cellar. Our conversation was fun and stress-free—nothing like the last time I'd been down there with Herb. We laughed a lot and talked about our kids. Thomas was struggling with his son, who had been getting in trouble with the police for years for petty theft. He hadn't graduated from high school, and Thomas constantly bailed him out of trouble. At twenty years old, he'd just recently moved out of Thomas's condo and was renting an apartment with his girlfriend. I nodded a lot, sympathizing, but my kids were so much younger—and they were girls. I had no experience I could draw from for advice, but it didn't really matter. Though we were talking about our lives, the conversation didn't feel heavy. We were both just enjoying each other's company.

On one of the nights Herb and I were on the phone, he started talking about women he was interested in at work. We'd been separated for more than three months, and I wasn't jealous. I no longer wanted to be with Herb. In a way, it had been easy to fall out of love with him because he'd committed the biggest sin against me by lying. I decided that him seeing other people could only be for the best: he'd retreat further from my life and, I hoped, find some happiness for himself in the process.

"If you want to go out and have fun, go ahead," I said. "I think I'm going to."

"Yeah?" Herb asked. "Are you seeing someone?"

"There's a guy at work," I said. "Maybe I'll see him. I don't know."

I was purposefully vague with Herb. Though it didn't bother me that he might ask someone out, I was uncomfortable being as open with that part of my life. He'd already told me he'd hit his first wife; maybe unconsciously I was thinking about that. I wasn't scared, but I realized how much he had kept from me, and I didn't want to hear anymore.

"Huh." Herb was silent a moment. "Well, good luck with that."

Though I played it cool with Herb and kept it together for the girls, I was struggling. My hurt wasn't that I couldn't live without him; it was that my whole marriage with him had been lies. I cried in bed at night, never so aware as then of how my life had changed. I needed an escape, a temporary lightening of the unhappiness I was bearing. I found it through Thomas.

We started seeing each other at the end of April, talking on the phone almost every night and spending our days off together at my house when the girls were in school. Things escalated quickly after we kissed for the first time, and soon we were having sex two or three times a day. It was so easy for me to just enjoy the pleasure and ignore the still-raw hurt of my breakup.

Thomas was well aware of what was going on with Herb. A few times he pointed out that I was on the rebound, or may have been "using" him, but the truth was I was an escape for him, too. He was burned out with work and struggling with his son. He'd planned to sell his condo and move to Arizona to care for his aging mother. We talked about such things without trouble; where Herb was closed, Thomas was open. It was easy between us; it always is when you're going through a hard time and look for something—or someone—else to fulfill your needs. This time, though, I knew I was the one who was guarded. Divorcing Herb was a wound far from healing.

"So how did your date go?" Herb asked one night. The words were nonchalant, but his voice was prickly.

"It was fine. He was a perfect gentleman." It was after ten o'clock, and I was on the phone in the bedroom. I only talked to Herb when the kids were in bed. To change the subject, I asked, "Did you ask your friend out?"

"Yeah," he said sullenly. "But it didn't happen. We're having all these conversations and then she tells me she has a boyfriend. She said the only reason she's with him is because she needs a place for her dog."

I winced. "Well, at least now you know."

It didn't strike me as odd until afterward that Herb had asked how my date with Thomas had gone; I hadn't told him I had actually *gone* on the date, only that I was thinking about it. He had probably just made an assumption. Still, I felt a quick flash of unease.

Thomas was supportive about my trying to maintain a friendship with Herb; he never acted jealous or made demands. For the most part, the time we spent together remained easy and fun. He came over often, and we watched movies with the kids in the living room. He got along great with the girls, especially Liza. Seeing her so open and friendly with him was surprising, almost jarring, after her years of rejecting Herb. Most days, Thomas went home after dinner, but he occasionally spent the night.

"I took my condo off the market," he said one night. "I don't want to move to Arizona anymore."

"Thomas!" I protested. "I don't want you to do that. Not for me, anyway."

"Well, we're having a good time, aren't we? We're good together."

"Yeah, of course we're having a good time. But, Thomas, I don't want to be a part of that decision. I want you to do what you need to do."

His action overwhelmed me. I wasn't even fully divorced yet; I couldn't be a part of the choices someone else was making for his future. My heart knew this wasn't a long-term thing, and I hadn't realized until then how reckless I was being with his emotions. Thomas wasn't my knight in shining armor, as sweet as he was and as much as he tried. Did such a thing even exist? I had no idea anymore.

One day, we were on my back deck, which overlooked a row of beautiful, huge pines on my property.

"Those trees have got to go," Thomas said, congested with allergies.

"What?" I was taken aback, looking from the trees to Thomas. "Herb and I built the deck around these trees. I love them."

"I have such bad allergies," Thomas said. "When this

is my house, we're going to cut those down."

"It ain't going to be your house," I snapped as I walked back inside.

It was a non-incident, really, but it heightened my awareness that Thomas and I wanted different things. He was talking about moving in, and I hadn't even told anyone at work we were seeing each other. Could I get to that point with him? I liked him, but I didn't think so. I knew I would have to end things soon but didn't know how.

Around the same time I was grappling with reality, I kept seeing what I thought was the same falcon. Always in the same area, always perfectly still as I drove past; I was coming to feel superstitious about it, as though it might mean something. Over a four-week period, I saw it five or six times, including once with the girls in the car. I'd taken them shopping in West Lebanon and on the way home said, "If we see the falcon, let's make that a sign that we need to save some money and go on a family vacation." We drove by the area where I always saw it, but the tree was empty. Then, a little farther up, I glanced out my window and the damn thing was there.

"Look, look!" I cried. "Girls, do you see the falcon?"

They were listening to their music, talking, not paying attention, but I was so excited. I felt that seeing the same falcon in the same area again and again had to mean something.

The last time I saw it, I was returning from the grocery store. The falcon flew right over my windshield, casting a shadow across my lap, and landed in a tree in my yard. We'd had a late snow, so the grass was green but dusted with white when I got out of my car. I walked over to the tree.

"Why are you following me?" I asked the bird. "What have you got to tell me?"

The falcon flew right past me and then away.

I emailed my sister, who was in Ireland, and asked what this sort of thing could mean. She was well read in mythology and symbolism, and I thought she might be able to give some insight. "It means change is coming," she said.

Change is coming. I wanted to believe that, and I did. The air around me felt electric.

In the last week of May, nearing my birthday, I took a few days off work. Thomas and I cleared out a space in the front yard and bought some manure so I could start a garden; I'd missed the garden season the year before. Gardening grounded me. There was something about digging, planting, and growing that made me feel more at peace. Over those few days, I planted green beans, cucumbers, tomatoes, squash, lettuce, potatoes—I envisioned the vegetables growing, the satisfaction of pulling them from the ground.

Herb called me that week. "I want to tell you that I saw a lawyer today."

Instantly my hackles rose. "What? Why?"

"I think you owe me at least thirty thousand more for the equity in those houses."

"Herb, I can't get thirty thousand for you—you knew that when you left. Six weeks have passed since we filed. We've already put all this on paper."

"Well, I'm going to make changes to our agreement."

"What's gotten into you?" I asked. "Why are you stirring the pot like this?"

"It's not fair. I want more money," he said coldly.

The line was silent as I gripped the phone, blood rushing to my head. I made myself speak calmly. "Go ahead. Get a lawyer. Talk to me through him."

○ ○ ○

By early June, I'd received paperwork in the mail from Herb's lawyer, and I had consulted an attorney of my own. I couldn't believe our divorce had taken this turn, but I would see it through as best I could.

Meanwhile, my feelings for Thomas started to shift. He'd made my birthday so much fun with the kids, taking us out to dinner and baking a cake that we all enjoyed. His dynamic with the girls was comfortable and warm, and both had taken to him in a way they never had with Herb. Maybe this *was* something more than just a fling, I thought. Maybe I *could* actually be with him long-term.

Late one night, I lay in bed staring through darkness at the ceiling. Thomas was turned toward me. I could feel him gazing at me. Softly, I said, "I think I'm falling in love with you."

There was a long, uncomfortable silence in which the only movement in the room was our chests as we breathed. Minutes passed. Thomas didn't respond. I squeezed my eyes shut so I didn't have to see him see me crying.

"Don't cry," he said.

I was at least mature enough to realize that it wasn't real love if it wasn't reciprocated, but I felt like a rejected teenager. What was wrong with me? How had I gone from having my life together to this—this falling-apart woman? I turned around and gave Thomas my back, crying myself to sleep.

I tried to keep my focus off negative things by buying

an astrology book. I had always been interested in astrology, and I was more deeply in need of understanding than I'd ever been. I combed through the pages of the thick, blue-covered book and seized on the fact that my moon was in the tenth house; according to the book, I had that in common with many celebrities. *I'm going to be famous!* I told myself, only half-joking. The thought had never crossed my mind, though for some reason now it rang true. I went out that day and bought lottery tickets. I didn't realize then how all of my actions were out of desperation—for a reason as to why my life had crumbled the way it had and for the promise of a better future.

One day, while the kids were in school, I fell to the floor of my bedroom in frustration and sadness. I didn't know where to look anymore. Something strange was happening, but I didn't know what it was. I'd never been so confused before. It surprised me that I was behaving the way I was; I felt as if I had no control. "Do with me what you want," I sobbed out loud. "I just want to find happiness. I give you my life. Put me in the direction you think I need to go."

CHAPTER 7

FIRE
WITHIN

JUNE 9, 2007, WAS A GLOOMY, DRIZZLY SATURDAY.
It was the first day of the kids' summer break, and they
slept in while I went to the farmers' market. My nursing friend Mary and I wandered around the stalls while
rain-burdened clouds hung overhead. I found some
unique things I hadn't bought in a while—homemade
Thai noodles, elk burgers—and we returned home. My
garden was stirring to life, and Mary gave me a basil
plant, asking me to grow it for her. I promised to plant
it with the rest of my seeds.

The balance of the day was ordinary. I cooked Thai
noodles for the kids and talked on the phone with Thomas.
I hadn't seen him since the night I'd told him I was falling in love. He wanted to see me that weekend, but I told
him my sister was coming into town. I was starting to
put distance between us.

After I hung up, I went to say goodnight to the girls.
It was ten o'clock and they asked if I was going to bed.

"Yeah," I told them. "I have to work in the morning.
Don't forget Kess gets in tomorrow."

Kess had just turned forty and was ready to leave Los
Angeles. She thought maybe she'd go to Portland, Maine,
and find a job there. In the meantime, she would be staying

with us, possibly as long as a month. She'd been sched-uled to show up that day, but travel plans had changed and she wouldn't arrive until the next. That was too bad, I thought, as I had to work.

I kissed Liza and Hannah goodnight. Then I went to my room and settled into the bed Herb and I had shared not long ago.

It was his birthday that day, and a little voice had been nagging me to call him but we weren't speaking. Plus, I reminded myself, he hadn't called me for my birthday ten days earlier. So, ignoring the voice, I turned off the light and quickly slid into sleep.

Around two thirty or two forty-five, I startled awake to a loud, shattering noise. It was like dozens of vases falling off a shelf, breaking. The house shook, and my first thought was that it was an earthquake. *No*, I thought, disoriented. *I'm not in California. I'm in Vermont.*

Groggily, I climbed out of bed and opened my bedroom door. Then I stopped. Just beyond me, in the living room, a man was stooped low to the ground. He was dressed all in black, and I couldn't make out his face in the darkness. *I'm being robbed*, I thought. But again, I was in calm, rural Thetford—not Los Angeles. None of it made sense, and I couldn't tell if I was in a dream. "Take whatever you want," I said, half-believing that my own voice would wake me.

He lunged toward me and I screamed, adrenaline rush-ing as I ran back into my bedroom. He caught me and his fist slammed into my face, knocking me to the floor. I tried to fight him as he ripped off my tank top and underwear. That was when I saw his eyes.

"Herb!" I yelled. "What are you doing? It's me, it's Car-men! What are you doing?"

Even as he punched me, I couldn't believe that Herb was doing this—not to *me*. I wanted to shake him, wake him from whatever trance he was in, and say, "Wait a minute, get yourself together, you don't do this stuff. This is *Carmen*!" He loved me, and we'd had many happy years together. I kept thinking something was wrong with him. I couldn't reason past my disbelief.

He walked a few feet away as, stunned, I tried to get my bearings. When he turned, both hands were wrapped around a baseball bat. He looked ready to hit a homerun. I was in shock: he was going to *hit me with a bat*? Sure enough, he swung at my head, and I threw my left arm up to block the blow. There was a crack as the bat made contact with bone. *My arm broke*, I thought matter-of-factly, but it didn't hurt in the moment. Herb swung over and over again, and I blocked it with the same arm at least three times before falling to the floor, woozy from being hit in the head.

"Is this worth the thirty thousand dollars to you?" he asked. It was the first time he'd spoken that night, and his voice was tinged with smugness.

"No," I said, just before losing consciousness. "I'll give you what you want, just please stop."

I came to as Herb was dragging me through the house. I could hardly see through the swelling in my eyes and face. I knew what had happened—I knew he was attacking me—and I yelled to the girls, "Lock yourselves in the bedroom and call the police!"

They told me later that they'd heard the big bang and it had taken them a minute to emerge from their rooms. Herb had been in my bedroom with the door closed when they came out, so they didn't know what was going on—only that I was moaning his name, pleading. When I yelled at them, they grabbed the phone and fled to their bathroom, the only room in the house with a lock.

Herb dragged me into Liza's room on the other side of the house. He stood me up, and I realized with horror that my hands were tied behind my back. Catching a glimpse of Liza's window, I briefly considered running through it but feared either the glass wouldn't break or it would kill me. Then Herb shoved me, knocking me off balance. The surface of Liza's dresser filled what sight I had left as I flew toward it; I had never felt more helpless, knowing I could do nothing to stop the impact. I smashed face-first into the dresser and fell to the ground again.

"I don't know why you're doing this!" I cried as he pummeled my back and ribs with the baseball bat. My body pulsated with pain.

He grabbed my throat and squeezed so hard I thought I was going to pass out. Just before I did, he let go. "If you shut up, I will stop hitting you," he said, as conversationally as if we were at the grocery store. The sheer normalcy of his voice—recognizing he was stone-cold sober—chilled me.

"Okay," I said, but the next thing I remember, he took the end of the bat and began raping me from behind. He shoved it deeply up my rectum, trying to force it all inside, but it was too big, of course. Then he pulled it out and did the same to my front side. The pain was nauseating, the shock overwhelming, and I screamed for him to stop, but he didn't. I lost consciousness again.

At one point, I looked over my shoulder and saw the girls in the doorway. Liza was on the phone, and Hannah held a ten-inch kitchen knife in her hand. Her face was frozen with terror. I was so scared Herb would take the knife and hurt them that I started screaming, "Get away! Just get out of here. Go get help. Don't get within reach of him!"

They ran, and when I regained consciousness, Herb was trying to knock down the bathroom door. I couldn't see through the swelling, but I knew the girls were on the phone. Herb spoke for the third time, commenting, "Well, I guess the police are coming."

"Are you going to run away?" I said. "Now is the time to go."

He didn't respond. Instead, he left the room and returned with a dish detergent bottle. It was filled with a thick, clear gel. He squirted it all over my face and body, and I spit out what had gotten into my mouth. It tasted bitter, like medicine.

"What is that?" I asked desperately. "What are you doing?"

I thought it was some kind of accelerant, that he was going to light me on fire, that I would never see my girls again. *Please,* I thought. I fainted, waking up when I heard, "This is the Vermont State Police. Come out with your hands up."

With no fight, Herb showed his hands and walked out.

"Come and get me!" I screamed. "I'm tied up, you need to come and get me!"

I was burning from the inside out, my fair skin darkening with irregular patches of brown. The officer yelled for me to hold on as he secured Herb and took him outside, laying him flat on the grass. Then he came and released my hands. I could barely see, I couldn't stand, and it was hard to crawl because I couldn't lower my left arm, but—using my right arm and my knees—I crawled out of the bedroom, down the little hallway, and yelled to Liza for water. She brought me a glass, but I couldn't do anything with it.

"I am so hot," I said, pulling myself into their bathroom. "I have to go in the shower. Girls, come in with me. Put the water on cold."

"All the way cold?" Liza asked.

"All the way." I struggled into the tub, and the icy water felt so good against my hot, hot skin. For ten or fifteen minutes, I was comfortable, and the girls stayed with me.

"Are you guys okay?" I asked, and they assured me they were.

I talked to them for a little while, until the policeman said from outside the bathroom, "The ambulance will be coming soon."

"But I need get to the hospital quickly!" I said. "Please, isn't there a helicopter?"

"I'm sorry, but it's too foggy out."

"Okay," I replied, and then assured the girls I was going to be okay.

"I know," Liza said.

"I'm going to be okay. I'm going to be okay."

"Mom, I know," she repeated.

"Call Kathie and Bill, and stay with them until things are worked out. Don't worry. I'm going to be okay."

"Mom, I *know*," she said. "You keep saying that. I heard you. I know."

I tried to rinse out my eyes, but my long hair had so much of the gel in it that it had spread quickly over my face. By the time the ambulance arrived, I had lost my sight completely.

I was helped out of the tub and onto the stretcher, and my left leg felt broken as the ambulance technicians bundled me up. Quickly, the eerie, unstoppable inside-out burning feeling started again, and the idea of the fifteen-minute ride to the hospital was overwhelming. Though I was awake, I don't remember the ride. One of the EMTs later told me, "You were talking to us the entire time. You were really concerned about your kids."

At the hospital—the same hospital where I worked—I was washed in water so cold it made me cry. I recognized the voice of one of the doctors I knew, and I called out his name.

"Todd?" I said. "Todd, is that you? Todd, are you here?"

"Yes, Carmen. I'm doing my ER rotation," he said. "I'm going to take care of you."

I was so happy to know somebody there.

After that, I remember being given some medicine—fentanyl or morphine—that took away a lot of my pain. I was completely blind by then, and I knew it wasn't from facial swelling; my left eye was swollen from Herb's fists, but I should still have had sight in my right eye. I didn't. And I had tasted what Herb had poured on me. I knew it was chemical and that I was burned. I was told I had to go to Boston for treatment, but I didn't want to leave my children.

At some point, Kathie came into the room with the girls. The doctor was not going to allow my children in, but Kathie—who, like me, had worked with him as a nurse—told him, "You have to let these girls in to see their mother because if she doesn't live, they'll never get to say goodbye."

When they entered the room, I said, "Everything is

going to be okay. Kathie, where is Hannah?"

"She's right here."

I stuck out my hand and grabbed Hannah's little fingers; both she and Liza were wearing gloves.

"It's going to be okay," I told them.

There had been a moment, that split-second I thought Herb was going to light me on fire, that I thought I might die. When I woke up, even through the pain, I was so happy to be alive that the thought of dying never occurred to me again. That was why I kept repeating, "I am going to be okay. No matter what, I am going to be okay." I didn't want the girls to worry. In retrospect, I must have believed that if I woke up after that moment, I was going to live. Period.

The ambulance ride to Boston is vague. At one point, I had one of the drivers call Kathie to make sure my kids were okay. By then, it was ten or eleven o'clock in the morning, and they had gone to her house.

Kathie said, "Tell her that they're sleeping and they're okay."

In the hospital, I was taken up to the ICU. The team there knew I was a nurse, and I spoke to them as they took care of me. Two of them—Chris and Joy—gave me a whirlpool bath. They told me they were going to induce a coma.

"I am going to put you to sleep, Carmen," Chris said. "We'll see you in about four months."

Through the shock and drugs and blindness, I said, "Can you make it just two?" It sounded like a joke, but I was devastated at the thought of not seeing my kids for that long. Still, the fear of death did not enter my mind. I knew, without a doubt, that I would wake from whatever strange dreams the next months would hold.

CHAPTER 8

LIMBO

"I LOST IT," READ THE HEADLINES. "I JUST LOST IT."

It was what Herb told the police that night. Over the next few weeks, as I slept and surgeons labored over dozens of surgeries to graft skin over my burns, the media covered my story. Newspapers from Thetford to LA talked about how Herb had broken into my home and attacked me with a baseball bat before severely burning me. They quoted burn experts, my doctors, and—more rarely—my family. Though I had told my girls I would be okay, no one knew for sure whether I would survive. Or, if I did, what my quality of life would be.

The chemical Herb had poured on me was industrial-strength lye. He'd bought it the week before at the local Home Depot. Herb knew exactly what it did and how dangerous it was; we had used it several times to unclog the drain in our house in Hawthorne. He always made sure the girls and I were nowhere nearby when the chemical was released. He said his intention that night was to attack Thomas, not me. He was going to hurt Thomas in front of me. What he actually did, he claimed, was never his plan.

Nobody believed him. I lived out in the country. If Thomas were at my house, his truck would have been in the driveway. Herb could have been under no illusion that he was there.

While I was in a coma, my family stepped in to cover my responsibilities. Kathie and Bill took care of the girls, making sure they still went to the lake, the mall, and friends' barbeques; the goal was to keep their lives as normal—and as busy—as possible.

My brother had recently moved out to Colorado for tattooing school, so my sister-in-law juggled all my finances: regular bills, two mortgages, collecting rent. And my mother and father acted as my representatives in court during Herb's arraignments.

He was initially charged with burglary, aggravated assault, and domestic assault. Before Herb hurt me, my parents' relationship with him was very good. After we moved to Vermont, my mother wrote him a letter, out of the blue, thanking him for being a good stepfather. *You see?* I used to tell him. *You just don't give yourself enough credit.* (At the time she wrote that, she didn't realize how unplugged he was from the girls.) My dad also liked Herb. When I had to work the previous Thanksgiving and the girls were spending the holiday with their father, my dad called Herb to see if he wanted to spend the day with him and his wife. My family may not have been one cohesive unit, but they welcomed Herb into what we did have.

After the attack, Herb never said anything to my family, and they each had a different interpretation of how he looked in court. My mother saw confusion, anguish, and sorrow on his face. My father and brother thought his expression was snide. I thought it was interesting how the women saw pain, while the men saw hate. Likewise, my father and brother were much angrier than my mother and sister.

In the first weeks though, my mother was consumed with thoughts of revenge. She woke up in the middle of the night and imagined taking a gun into the next hearing and shooting him. It was the only way she could cope. It was easier to think about Herb than it was to think about me.

It ended when she got up early one morning thinking again about how she could hurt him. She spent time with a girlfriend that day, and they ran into a man they knew at the grocery store. He told them how everyone in town wanted Herb dead and how all anyone could think and talk about was how they would cause him pain if they had the chance. Mom realized then that everyone was reacting to the violence he'd shown with thoughts of more violence, and it suddenly made no sense to her at all. Why would they want to do to him what he'd done to me? Why would everyone want to be as inhumane as he was? She returned to *Conversations with God,* a book she'd read years before, and turned to the chapter on forgiveness. She thought, *If I can, I ought to do this, because I can't think of my grandkids or Carm with all my thoughts of him.* For her, even if no one else could understand, forgiveness was a road back to sanity.

When I was stable, Kathie brought the girls to the hospital every Sunday. I can only imagine what they saw when they looked at me—I was a patchwork of bandages and skin grafts, with almost nothing left of me to recognize. In the beginning, doctors used cadaver skin to cover my open wounds. Though it would eventually flake and fall off, its purpose was to serve as a blanket of sorts, temporarily staving off infection by keeping the wounds closed. Later, they harvested skin from my shins, one of the few places on my body that hadn't been burned. Like grating a slice of cheese from a block, they removed the top level of healthy skin and used it to cover the open areas. They waited a week before doing it again. Eventually, skin from my shins covered most of my legs; I had a tattoo above my right ankle, and pieces of it ended up on the back of my left thigh.

Only my hands and feet looked normal, though they, too, were marred: at some point, Herb had bitten so deeply into my fingers that they required stitches. Among all the other injuries I suffered, the "fight bites" were perhaps paid least attention, but to think of Herb *biting* me—it was animalistic and savage. I have no memory of that, but at least it means I fought hard. Soon, the skin of my hands was smooth and unscathed once more.

As I slept, the girls worked through their own memories and emotions surrounding what had happened—not just the attack but also the complicated lenses through which they had seen Herb. Kathie found a counselor for each of them, who later asked that they write out some of their feelings.

Liza wrote, "I didn't like him. I didn't want him around. It was really awkward. My mom never realized this. He asked us one day—always when Mom was at work—he asked us if we liked him. We sat in silence and then Hannah left. I told him it was awkward to be put on the spot.

"I'm surprised how much my mom didn't realize," she continued. "Maybe she would have done something if [she had known] we were miserable. Maybe we didn't tell Mom about Herb because he lived with us since we were little. Maybe if I had said something, maybe he would have tried [to make things work]. Maybe he would have been devastated and left, but then he would have left because of me."

Of the divorce, Hannah wrote, "Mom was sitting on the couch. Liza was on the computer. It was quiet. Mom burst out crying. I said, 'Sorry.' I didn't want to say, 'Oh, well,' because I knew it was hard for Mom. Liza was home alone when he moved out. He came up to her and said, 'I'm sorry I wasn't a good father to you.' Liza said, 'OK.'"

Both girls were awake when Herb threw a ten-pound weight through the sliding glass doors that night. Liza had drunk two orange Powerades and was still feeling the sugar rush. She and Hannah were on the computer and watching TV, and they exchanged puzzled glances when the crash shattered the early morning silence. Then they heard me scream. They rushed out of their room to see that my door was closed. I yelled for them to call the police, and they heard me cry out, "Herb!" before locking themselves in the bathroom.

"I was sitting at the edge of the tub, and Hannah was leaning against the door," Liza wrote.

"And then we hear Mom moaning, 'Herb, Herb, stop,' and Liza says [to the dispatcher], 'Herb's here, they're getting divorced.' I was feeling terrified," Hannah wrote. "Herb was a big guy. He's like six feet, two hundred and fifty pounds. Mom is like five feet four inches, shorter than me, and a hundred and thirty pounds."

"Then Herb broke the door," Liza wrote. "I looked at my sister's face and she screamed."

"I knock off his glasses because he's like blind and can't see without his glasses. And he punches me on my face. It was under my right eye, like a little red mark, like a cut that lasted for two days," Hannah wrote.

"I looked into my mom's room and I had tunnel vision," Liza wrote. "I was still in the bathroom, I have no idea where Herb was. My bedroom light was still on and I could see Mom. I was looking at an angle. I don't remember if she was looking at me. I don't know if she was hurt. She was on her knees and her hands were behind her back—I figured she was tied. I had an adrenaline rush for most of the time. I never had the feeling that she was going to be killed. I was probably worried and angry because the police weren't there yet."

"Herb took Mom to Liza's room. [Liza] runs to the kitchen and grabs a knife. Me and Liza were shouting, 'Don't hurt her, don't touch her, she didn't do anything to you!' I was thinking, *This is so unfair.*"

"My sister took [the knife] from me and said she was going in," Liza wrote. "I remember watching her. She opened the door [a few inches] and just stood there, she froze."

"Mom was down on her knees. Herb was reaching for the door and I realized he had pushed all of Liza's furniture in front of it. I was really confused because I didn't know what he was doing to her. He sees the knife in my hand so he shuts the door completely. He puts more stuff in front of it."

"I told my sister we needed to go outside. When Hannah started throwing things against the window I did too, and I put the knife down. We were looking for it and that's when the blinds hit the window. It went silent a couple of times."

"Even the dogs stopped barking from next door."

"We didn't know what he was doing. The feelings were upsetting and frightening. I said we needed to go to the road, in case he comes from the side of the house. Before we got to the road, Hannah said that if Mom dies, she would kill herself. I said, 'No, you're not, Mom's not going to die.'"

"We were waiting in the street and a car passes by and we didn't touch it, but we were like, 'Are you gonna stop?' If I had been the person driving the car, I would have stopped. Then we saw another car coming and we said, 'It better be the cop,' and it was. And he had his gun drawn. I was like, 'I hope he shoots him.' He never went into the hallway. He was in the living room, and he said, 'Thetford Police' and then 'Please come out with your hands up' and that kind of stuff. I saw Herb come out with the cop dude. And then he was laying on the ground handcuffed."

"The officer said if he does anything, scream."

"And the cop ran back to see if anyone was in there."

"The officer came back out and said tell them we need an ambulance. I told the operator and she asked what happened. Herb said, 'You can tell them I acid-piped her.' It made him sound proud of himself. Hannah yelled, 'Fuck you! All she wanted was a normal life after you!'"

"After that the cop said, 'You need to go in there and tell your mom she's gonna be okay.' We both ran in and saw her crawling out of Liza's room, and we were like, 'Oh, Mom, Mom,' and she was like, 'I need water.' I don't remember what she looked like. I was in complete shock."

"The blanket that Kathie made me was ruined with blood and acid. Mom was brown and I think she had raspberries all over her arm. Her eye and lip were swollen and black. You could tell—her body was brown but I wasn't thinking of that. All she said was that she couldn't see and she was burning and she needed to get in the shower."

"She said, 'Okay, girls, I'm going to be in the hospital for a couple of weeks and I need one of you to do something really disgusting for me.' Liza says, 'What, Mom?' It was so like Mom. Mom was kind of laughing. It was the last time I heard her laugh and it was her voice. Now her voice is different. 'I need one of you to take out my tampon.' Liza smiles and says, 'After you, Hannah.' So I do it. It was just like an automatic thing. I wasn't thinking or feeling."

"She told me to call Kathie and Bill Demers," Liza wrote. "I said 'What's the number?' She said it's on the phone. I went into her room but I didn't turn the light on. I only noticed her change cup was knocked over. I told Kathie that Mom was hurt and she needed to meet us at the hospital. The first ambulance was just a guy in a station wagon. Then the real ambulance and fire trucks came.

"I didn't think he would kill her," Liza continued. "She's too strong for that. I think he wanted to torture Mom … slow and painful and that's what he did, but he didn't kill her. After it happened, it seemed like a dream to me—not real."

 ° ° °

Nothing must have seemed real during the first month I was in a coma. Either that, or things seemed far too real. Fifteen minutes of Herb's fury had altered the course of my family's lives, and it was still unclear what direction that course would take.

In late June, a couple of visitors tried to help my family answer that question. Their names were George and Mike, and both were burn survivors.

George had been thirty, with a wife and two little boys,

when he got burned in the 1970s. He was pulling up the floor in his kitchen, and the pilot light on the stove hadn't been turned off. It ignited on the chemicals George was using and blew him right out of the house. He was eighty-five percent burned. Fortunately, the second-degree burns on his face healed over time. His worst scarring was hidden beneath his clothes.

His friend Mike, who was from Boston, was not so lucky. He was celebrating the Red Sox win in the World Series, had too much to drink, and was in a car accident, during which flames ate his skin from the waist up. He lost his nose, an ear, and an eye and gained tremendous scarring.

A social worker at the hospital had set up the meeting between George and Mike and my mother, father, sister, and Dr. Watkins, who worked in the trauma, burns, and surgical critical unit. George was a volunteer for the Phoenix Society for Burn Survivors, and Mike had been a patient at Brigham and Women's Hospital as well. Both often talked to patients suffering from similar injuries, as well as their families. They knew firsthand the life-long effects of these injuries; only so much scarring is physical. The rest, the emotional damage, is often even harder to treat.

When Mike walked into the meeting room, my mother tried not to show how startled she was at his disfigure-ment. They sat down around a small table, and George and Mike told the group about their experiences. It was the first time my family had met anyone who had endured injuries similar to mine.

"It's going to be okay," Mike said. "Everything you're feeling—the anger, the fear—is totally normal."

"No matter what, there's support out there," George

added. "We know a lot of people who have been in Carmen's situation, and they don't just 'make it through.' They have relationships. They lead good lives. It's possible."

Kess and Mom exchanged glances. My injuries were so severe that no one had dared offer what these two men were giving them: hope.

"I want to do my part to be there for Carm," Kess said. "What can I do?"

Kess and I didn't have a close relationship at that point. Though she was only fourteen months older than I was, we'd been on and off our whole lives. When we were off, we weren't necessarily fighting; we simply weren't close. It seemed, though, that any time we went through some big crisis or joy, our lives paralleled and we drew closer. Maybe this would be one of those times.

"That's a wonderful question," George said. "The truth is that a lot of burn survivors lose people they had in their lives, especially if they're disfigured. The more you can do to support your sister, both physically and emotionally, the better. We have monthly meetings that might help you do that."

Kess nodded. "I'll be there."

After George and Mike left, my family felt more positive than they had since I'd been hurt. If it were possible to survive something like this and still lead a happy, fulfilling life, they thought I would do it. They let themselves believe.

° ° °

While I was asleep, my friends and family held dozens of fundraisers for me. Two friends from high school, Mary and Jill, opened a bank account under my name, letting people know where to donate. My dad—against my family's wishes—updated the media frequently about my condition. He wanted people to know what had happened and how I was doing, so that they could support me. As a result, he got calls often from people who wanted to host dinners and events for me, and he went to as many of them as he could. There were a lot of spaghetti dinners in those days.

In July, my blood pressure dropped to sixty over forty, and my body was rampant with infections. Most burn victims don't die from the wounds themselves; they die from infection. Dr. Watkins called a meeting with my family. My parents, sister, sister-in-law, and Kathie and Bill anxiously gathered around him.

"I'm not going to sugarcoat this," he said. "This is very serious. She can't sustain a blood pressure this low for long, or her organs will begin failing."

"Is she going to be okay?" my mother asked. They were in a separate meeting room at the hospital, where the family often gathered for doctors' briefings.

"We'll know in the next twenty-four to forty-eight hours." He added, "She'll either improve, or she won't."

Herb and I signed my living will in January 2007, just as our fighting began. Bill told me he thought it was strange I was making a will at thirty-eight years old. I understood. No young person wants to make a living will; it forces us to think of our own mortality, and we simply don't see life in that way yet. I told him, though, that it was for the girls.

In the will, I specified that Kathie would make any major decisions regarding my medical care if I were incapacitated. I also checked the box indicating that I didn't want extreme measures taken to save my life; if I crashed in the next couple of days and couldn't immediately be resuscitated, they were to let me go.

Later, my family told me how terrifying that meeting with the doctor was; everyone knew this was the time I was either going to live or die, and what thread of hope they had felt one tiny snip away from breaking.

Kess stayed later than everyone else that night, and a nurse gave her a piece of paper covered with numbers: my blood pressure, temperature, other vital statistics. "I'm not going to be in tomorrow morning," the nurse said, "so when you come in, compare her numbers with these. You'll be able to tell whether she's going up or down."

Kess had a heavy night in the small apartment she had rented near the hospital. She came back early the next morning, paper in hand. When she walked into my room, another nurse was already there. She smiled at Kess. "She's better today."

CHAPTER 9

LIFE
IS
A
CHOICE

WHILE LIFE WENT ON—FAMILY VISITS, COURT proceedings, surgeries—I dreamed.

I was surrounded by a group of people in dark clothes. Someone wanted to hurt me, and a gunshot's violent blast cut through the air. The group—or what felt like a gang—took me down to a cellar, and I realized they weren't people at all but shadows with no arms or legs. All I could see were the whites of their eyes and gleam of their teeth. One of them screamed at me, and my dream-body thrummed with fear.

In another dream—this is embarrassing but true—Dr. Phil McGraw's wife, Robin, told me they had broken up.

"You're kidding," I said. "That's terrible."

She said, "Well, not really. Everything is good, and I'm happy. He just needs a friend, Carmen, and I want you to go out to dinner with him."

"But, Robin, I'm all bandaged up," I protested. "I've gotten seriously hurt."

"I know, but we'll have a limo pick you up, and you

won't have to do anything. Just go to dinner."

Sure enough, a car picked me up with Dr. Phil inside. He was dressed in a long-sleeved blue oxford shirt, a dark blue suit jacket draped on the seat beside him. I thought, *Oh my God, it's Dr. Phil!* But without the jacket, he just looked like a regular guy going out to dinner.

We talked all through a fancy meal, until I left the table to go to the bathroom. Then I became disoriented, wandering through long wood-paneled hallways. There were no differentiating marks to help me back to the dining room, and every time I turned, it was into another hallway. I was tired and didn't feel well. Finally and inexplicably, I was back at the table.

"I think I got lost," I told Dr. Phil.

Then dinner was over and we walked outside, lowering ourselves into the limo to go home.

In my most vivid dream, I was talking to a disembodied voice that was mine but not-mine.

"You know, I don't really understand life," I said to the voice, sadly.

"Look at all the different doors," the voice said.

I looked, and around me stretched dozens of doors— one looked like a door on a country house, another as if it belonged to an apartment in the city—doors and more doors.

"So …," I said, considering. "You just pick the life you want?"

"Yes. That is what you do."

I glanced again at the doors, and they all shrank before me, becoming smaller and smaller until they combined into a ball of dust. The dust ball lay against a baseboard on a green and white striped kitchen floor. I stared at it and thought, *All of life is in that little ball.*

"Are you kidding me?" I asked.

The voice responded: "Life is a choice."

Then a large dark movie screen filled my vision. The word LIFE was spelled across it in big white letters. The screen blinked, and the word IS appeared. Another blink: A. The final blink: CHOICE. Life. Is. A. Choice.

"So ... life is a choice?" I repeated.

"Yes," the voice replied.

° ° °

In August 2007, two months after Herb attacked me, I began stirring from my coma. Though I knew what had happened to me, I wasn't completely lucid. My first words, which I wrestled out through the tracheotomy in my throat, were, "Hannah and Liza?"

Kess and Mom leaned in close to me, crying and laughing. It took them a long time to decipher what I was trying to say, but they were full of joy at this, my first sign of recovery.

As soon as they left the hospital, Kess called Hannah and Liza. They each picked up a different phone in Kathie and Bill's house. When Kess told them my first words, Hannah said, "So she said *my* name first?" All three of them burst out laughing at the classic Hannah moment.

I was slow to return completely, though. For the next month, I lived a half-dream that my father and brother had killed themselves. I talked out loud as I dreamed, telling Kess that I had gone to the barn where my brother had shot himself.

"I saw the blood," I said.

I didn't understand. Why would they take their lives

now? Could they simply not handle what had happened to me? It was hard to tell what was real and what wasn't. It was unsettling to wake up that way, and my memories of those first days come in brief, murky flashes.

Right before I became fully lucid, I spoke to my dad on the phone. "I thought you were dead!" I said, confused and not quite believing he wasn't.

On September 23, I woke up for real. Immediately, memories rushed: Hannah's premonition of "something bad" happening, her deep and terrible crying, the falcon and its omen of change, my desperate prayer for guidance, and the attack. Finally, I remembered my dream: life is a choice. The pieces crashed together.

My bed was in an upright position, and I couldn't move. Then I heard Kess's voice. "Hi, Carm," she said.

"Hi, Kess," I replied. My voice was clear and normal.

There was a full beat of startled silence. I couldn't see her, but Kess exchanged a dazed, dumfounded look with my nurse, Julie, who sat in a chair by my door. Julie returned the look with equal surprise, and Kess laughed and rushed to me.

"I've been down for quite a while," I said. "What is it—July?"

"No, Carm," Kess said, as though she'd answered this question before. "It's September."

"September!" I cried. "What day? I don't want to miss the kids' birthdays."

That was when Kess knew, absolutely, that I was back.

"It's only the twenty-third," she reassured me. She kept her voice calm and deliberate, which I appreciated. As a nurse, I'd seen families overjoyed at the outcome of an operation or test and then devastated when the patient, who might still be suffering, didn't share their enthusiasm. I knew Kess was happy that I was awake, but she didn't want to burden me with her excitement.

"Okay," I said. I had five days until Liza's birthday and ten until Hannah's. "I can't see. Do they have my eyes sewn shut?"

"Yes," Kess said.

"Am I going to be able to see again?"

"They think so."

"Okay," I said, quelling panic. After seeing for thirty-nine years, the prospect of being blind was horrifying, so I didn't let myself consider it.

I said to Kess, "I thought Donny and Dad killed themselves. I know now it was just a dream."

"Yes, it was," Kess said.

"Did they have to code me?"

"No. You had a bad twenty-four hours in July, but you made it through."

I sighed with relief. To me, life was worth fighting for, but only to a certain point. When Kess told me no one had intervened to save me, I felt certain that *I* had made that choice. My dream, I was sure, was the moment I had chosen to stay, and it had to be for a reason. It all did. With so little power over anything else, that conviction meant something to me.

Kess had started a CarePages website for me, a site where she updated friends and family on my progress. When I became lucid, Kess wrote, "Carm is back!"

She also started calling the family for me. I kept placing the phone on the left side of my head, and Kess kept moving it to the right. I was burned and stiff and couldn't raise my arms high enough to move the phone myself.

I finally said, exasperated, "Put it on the other side."

"I can't," Kess replied.

"I want it on my left, Kess."

"Carm, I *can't*—you don't have an ear there."

"Oh," I said. I didn't have an *ear?* I couldn't imagine what not having an ear was going to be like, but I pushed the thought aside because I wanted to talk to my family. "Okay," I said to Kess. Then I talked with the phone on my right.

After a while, if I lowered my head, I could raise my hands near my ears. My hands (and feet) felt normal, but I had nerve damage to my fingers. It was less severe on my left hand, so I used that one any time I wanted to feel something—like my ears. On the left side, I had only a loose flap of skin. Later, I'd joke around with the kids and Kess, flipping it around and saying, "This is my little ear." Eventually, my flippy little ear sank into my head, but the hole was closed the whole time; from the moment I awoke, I was deaf on that side.

I couldn't wait to talk to my girls, and I asked Kess to call them right away.

"I was scared you wouldn't be normal anymore," Liza confessed.

She had visited me before I was lucid and told me I'd said strange things when I tried to speak through my tracheotomy. I whined and wasn't myself. Once, I threw a tantrum, thrashing my arms and legs as best I could because I didn't want her to leave. Liza had said soothingly, as if I were a child, "It's okay, Mom. I'm going to be back. It's okay."

"That's part of waking up," I reassured her now. "I was confused because of all the drugs."

"Yeah, they might have told me that, Mom. But I was still scared."

Liza always took things so in stride that her worry surprised me. But then, a month of seeing your mother only half-lucid and not at all herself is probably a lifetime to a fourteen-year-old.

"Well, I'm back now," I said.

After Kess left, I spent the nighttime hours slipping uncomfortably down the bed. I couldn't find the nurse-call button and kept twisting sideways, sightless and confused. Still, at least I was lucid. I knew I was in the ICU and that nurses were nearby. I didn't want to be one of the screaming patients I'd heard throughout my career, so I tried to be polite when I called out, "Hello? Hello? Is anyone there?"

"Yes, Carmen," a nurse called back. "We're here. We'll help you out."

Thirst was a raging thing inside me. I was desperate for water, soda, anything, but I was only allowed to chew on ice chips so that I wouldn't aspirate. One afternoon when Kess was visiting and the nurse had left, I said, "Kess, I want to be bad. Give me that ginger ale!"

Kess laughed. "But, Carm, you haven't used a straw yet. You still have the trache hole in your throat! What happens if the soda goes into it?"

"I drown," I said matter-of-factly.

"Well, I'm worried, Carm. I'm not a nurse."

"I *am* a nurse," I said. "I'll tell you when to worry."

Kess and I laughed together, and she brought the soda over to me. I took the can and tried to chug it like a beer, spilling it all over my hospital gown. We giggled like kids the whole time, and I whispered, "Go get me a new johnny" so I wouldn't get in trouble with the nurses.

Once I started to eat solid food, the first meal I asked Kess to bring was raspberries and chocolate pudding. I had asked Andrea, another nurse, to set up a table for Kess with flowers and a tablecloth, and I'd dictated a note that said, "Kess, I appreciate everything you've done for me. Carm."

"What's all this?" Kess asked, her voice lifting with surprise.

"It's for you," I said. "You brought your lunch?"

"Yes, and yours."

"Well, you sit down and eat your lunch. Don't worry about me. I'll take care of feeding myself."

Kess started to protest, but I shushed her and accepted the dish of raspberries she handed me. I heard a chair scrape against the floor and imagined Kess sitting at the table. I hoped she'd have a chance, even a short one, to relax.

Fumbling, I tried to eat my raspberries. They either slipped from my fingers or out of my mouth, rolling all over my chest and the bed. Kess's chair again scraped the floor. "Sit!" I ordered. "Eat!"

"But—"

"Andrea," I said, "can you please feed me these raspberries?"

After Kess had finished her lunch, she sat beside me and spooned chocolate pudding into my mouth. After three months of being fed through tubes, it was the sweetest thing I'd ever tasted. "I love you," I told Kess between bites.

A week later, I was transferred from the ICU down to an inpatient unit where Kess was able to stay with me during the night. It was then that I started seeing people who didn't exist.

Every night, when Kess turned out the lights for bed, my vision swam with people I'd never seen before: an old-time Native American family staring at me soulfully, their shoulders and torsos draped with ponchos; a very old woman dressed in eighteenth-century garb, her skin deeply wrinkled and long gray hair held back in a low ponytail. Sometimes I didn't get a look at their faces, but I saw all types of people: white, black, redheaded, blonde. Some looked as if they could be alive now, others as if they had existed hundreds of years ago in far different places than the Upper Valley or even the U.S. Every time the lights turned off, I saw them—always different people, always briefly: thirty seconds here, a minute there. I knew it was my brain reacting to blindness, but I looked forward to the characters I'd see regardless. It was comforting, looking at people who looked back at me. I called them my angels.

One time, when the lights flicked on in the morning, eight or ten small children surrounded me. They were playing with a blue spongy ball. A little boy ran off with the ball, and a little girl with blonde hair and freckles came up to me with a beseeching, puppy-dog look that made me laugh.

"You're talking to your people again?" Kess teased.

I laughed back. "You should see what I'm seeing."

While the sedatives were still in my system, I didn't feel a lot of pain. Then, about ten days after I woke up, I did.

The dressing changes on my legs and chest took two hours. They started with being helped into the shower, which was exhausting because I couldn't see or walk, and

I had been down for so long that my muscles were weak beneath the burns. The water hit my wounds with a piercing, burning sensation, like being stuck with needles that didn't get pulled out. The head wounds were the worst. Sometimes, I didn't allow the nurses to use soap because it stung so badly. It was difficult to keep the wounds clean if my hair grew, so the nurses were instructed to cut it constantly—even an inch was too long. However, some of it poked through the wounds anyway, stabbing and reopening them. The pain when the nurses combed out the scabs was excruciating. Meanwhile, the tube feeding me through my nose kept hitting my stomach lining and making me sick, so I couldn't eat for the first week. All these challenges hit one after another.

I was so overwhelmed with pain that I didn't initially worry about what I looked like. I could tell I had my arms, legs, and feet. I knew I could speak and hear. Everything I needed, except my sight, seemed to be in place. But with my dressing changes stretching for hours, I started to wonder about my skin and my scars. I'd seen so many wounds in my career, and I tried to figure out which parts of my body were open. It was hard to tell. My nerve endings had been burned, so there was always a strange lack of sensation along with hypersensitivity—an unrecognizable pain. I had no clue what I looked like, and my immediate suffering took priority.

My attending physician was about thirty-two years old, and he was gone for two of the five weeks I was in rehab. When he *was* there, he talked to me three separate times about the dangers of becoming addicted to narcotics.

"Only take as much as you need," he advised.

Today I would have shot back, "Getting addicted to

painkillers when I'm more than eighty percent burned isn't my concern." But back then, nurse or not, I was vulnerable. I agreed when he opted to put me on methadone instead of other drugs.

The strongest pain medication I'd ever taken up to that point was Vicodin for a root canal, so my body was completely unaccustomed to this new drug. Immediately, I started hallucinating.

Kathie and Bill had brought the girls to visit, and Kess and my mother were there as well. I thought I was sitting, though I probably wasn't, and thought I saw a dozen Labrador retrievers trot into the room. They circled my family, and I told everyone, "Look! There's a dog next to you. Pet the dogs."

They all laughed, and Liza said, "Yep, Mom, I am petting the dog."

Then I said, "Look, Kess. Grammy's here."

Right in front of me was my dead grandmother. She looked the way she had when I'd last seen her, when she was in her seventies and before the Alzheimer's hit. She wore a black cardigan, unbuttoned, and a little hat, and she carried a pocketbook I'd never seen before.

"Hi!" I said. "Hi, Grammy!"

Her mouth wasn't moving, but I somehow knew she wanted Kess to hug her.

"Kess, stand up and give Grammy a hug," I scolded. The aware part of me knew none of this was happening, but I was *seeing* it, so I acted as if my grandmother were there. I didn't know what else to do.

"Okay, Carm," Kess said. Casting uncomfortable glances at the rest of my family, she stood and embraced the air.

Soon after that, the hallucinations worsened. I went

crazy with the methadone, believing things that weren't real, thrashing in bed, and yelling. Kathie and Bill stopped bringing the girls, and the doctors erected a nylon tent around my bed to keep me from tumbling over the metal railings. If visitors were in the room and I was calm, they could peel down one side of the tent to talk to me. Of course, the only visitors I had during that time were my mom and Kess.

"Carm, you are in a bed," Kess told me.

I heard her words but couldn't believe them. I thought I was in a car. Another time, I got so angry at my mother that I fired her. "You're not paying any attention to me. You keep going out smoking with the nurses; you couldn't care less, so you know what? You're fired."

The idea is funny now, but after all the pain and rage and fear she'd lived through in the previous few months, my remark was cutting.

Unlike my "angels," my methadone hallucinations weren't comforting. For one, they never stopped. I didn't know how to turn my internal gaze away, and the images were so vivid that I almost convinced my family that I had my sight—which was crazy because my eyes were still sewn shut. But they held up their fingers, and Kess said I guessed so accurately a lot of the time that they thought I could see through the little holes in my skin.

The whole five days I hallucinated, I was awake.

"Here," Kess kept saying. "Here's some medicine to help you sleep."

"No!" I said. "I won't take anything." I was desperate for this to end but didn't want to put something into my body that might make it last longer. Over and over again, I refused the sleeping pills.

In the most frightening hallucination, I could see my-self lying in bed—me as I used to look—working with the therapist. She was stretching out my arms and legs, and I looked down at both of us, observing my life from outside my own skin.

"I can see me," I told her. "I can see you."

"You're hallucinating," Kess said.

"I know," I said, exhausted, "but it's so hard for me to believe you. It's right here. It's so crystal clear. How can I not be seeing?"

As I spoke, I glimpsed myself in a different place in the room, sitting on a chair. The vision was jarring, dizzying. How could I be in the chair but also in bed? And who was *seeing* all this? That was the only me-body I couldn't see. I must have been floating. I was in three places at once, and it was clear as day.

That's the worst part about hallucinating when you're blind: what you're living is clearer than a dream, and you can't escape the dream by waking up. Nor can you escape what you're living by falling asleep. Closing my eyes wouldn't get rid of the images; my eyes were *already* closed! I couldn't just see black anymore. It was perma-nent wakefulness with no way of discerning between reality and fantasy. What if this never ended? What if I was caught forever in a realm of life no one else inhabited? The thought was terrifying, and the possibility of stopping my madness was worth the risk of the pills extending it. On the fifth day, I begged, "Just give me something. Give me something to make me sleep."

I took the medicine Kess offered, and—at last—my mind surrendered to a deep, dreamless sleep.

CHAPTER 10

HOMECOMING

DOCTORS HAD TOLD MY FAMILY THAT I WOULD BE in the hospital for nine months; that would put me in rehab until March of 2008. After the methadone experience, I couldn't imagine four more months of my life disappearing inside this hospital.

"I'm going home by Christmas," I declared to my mother and Kess. "I've already talked to the doctors, and they think that's doable."

Two weeks later, I changed it to Thanksgiving.

"Is that okay?" I asked my family.

No one wanted to upset me by disagreeing—that was one benefit of my injuries—but I knew they had legitimate concerns: who would take on my hours-long dressing changes or help me shower and dress? Who would guide me around the house? Who would cook and clean and get the girls to and from school? All the normal and numerous daily tasks we all take for granted were no longer an option for me. At least, not yet.

"I can't do the dressings for you," my mother said. "I can take care of the kids and the cooking, but I just can't do the dressings, Carm."

"That's okay, Mom," I said. "I understand."

I did understand. The task was so involved that I knew it would overwhelm my mother. The problem was that

I thought it would also overwhelm the visiting nurses, whose goal it was to train a family member anyway. I didn't know who else to ask. Kess was staying in Boston, applying for jobs. She'd come up to see me when she could, but she wouldn't be living with me the way my mother planned to. I felt at a stalemate.

Then, the next time Kess visited, she told me she hadn't yet gotten a job. I instantly felt it was meant to be.

"Why don't you come home with me?" I asked. "I can help with your bills, and you can help me with my dressing changes."

Reluctantly, she said, "Oh ... I don't know, Carm. I'm not a nurse."

"I'll teach you," I said.

Kess was quiet for a few moments. Was she looking at me, wondering if this was something she could physically and emotionally handle? I imagined her dark eyes serious as she weighed her options.

"Okay, Carm," she said. "I can do that. You'll just have to be patient with me."

The next major question—at least on everyone else's minds—was exactly where *home* would be. No one considered that I'd want to return to where we'd lived before, but I never thought twice about it. I had chosen that house. We had built a big deck out back and converted the basement into a family room for the kids. It was close to the kids' school, and it had enough space for Mom to take one bedroom, the girls to have their own, and Kess to sleep with me. If Liza and Hannah wouldn't be traumatized by going back, I thought we should. Why should we let one night—fifteen minutes of rage—take everything from us?

"Girls," I said, "I really want to go home. It's *our* home. How would you both feel about going back?"

There was a long silence. Hannah would follow Liza's lead, I knew.

"Okay," Liza finally said. "If that's what you want to do, we'll do it."

"If it ends up being too hard for us, we'll make a change. But let's see if it can work first."

Later, Thomas came to visit me in rehab. We had never put a label on our relationship before I got hurt, but he had somehow become my boyfriend while I was in my coma.

The week I woke up we were making arrangements for the girls' birthday party, and Kess asked if I wanted Thomas to be there.

"Why?" I asked.

"He's been around all summer. He really stepped in for the girls."

I shrugged. "Well, I guess it's fine."

The kids' party was in my room in the ICU. The nurses helped us get a cake and presents, and we sang a clumsy happy birthday. When Thomas got there, I shook his hand and thanked him for being there for Liza and Hannah. I appreciated that he hadn't walked away.

Two weeks later, Thomas wanted to come spend the weekend with me in the hospital. I told Kess I didn't want to do it. I was in no place to try for a relationship—especially one I had been on the verge of ending before all this happened.

"Carm, he really cares about you," Kess said gently. "You can't do this to him. He's been here for months—he wants to be with you. Besides, the girls want him around."

I softened when I thought of the girls. They had seen

us happy before I got hurt. They must have thought we were in love. For a while, I had, too. Exhausted, I agreed to see him.

That weekend, he stayed and helped with my care. It was humiliating. I had to use a bedpan, and he cared for me with the solicitude of the nursing assistant he was. "Thomas," I asked, "why are you still here?"

A few moments passed. "I couldn't say no to those kids."

I understood then why he had stayed: he had convinced himself it was the "right thing to do." He knew how people would look at him if he'd left me while I was burned and in a coma. So he convinced himself to stay, and I felt a similar pressure to keep him in my life. I was a mess, and Mom and Kess couldn't handle my care seven days a week. Plus, the girls had bonded with him. At that point, it seemed easier to let him stay than to make him leave.

It didn't take long for the pushy side of Thomas's personality to emerge again. "I want to change downstairs around at the house," he said one day at rehab.

I prickled. "You mean *my* house?"

"Right, just move things around a little."

"Leave it alone," I said. "Don't do anything until I get home."

I was territorial to begin with, but Herb had taken so much of my power that I needed to maintain control where I could.

"Do you hear me?" I said to Thomas, who hadn't responded.

"Yeah, Carm—I got it."

o o o

On November 19, 2007, I woke up with bubbling excitement: I was going home. I had only been in rehab for five weeks, but it seemed like so much longer since I had slept in my familiar bed, seen the towering pines out back, and walked down our long driveway to check the mail. The day had an air of festivity and anticipation.

A friend had given me a new green tracksuit, and I was eager to wear clothes beyond the tank top and underwear I lived in at rehab. I couldn't move my arms enough to put on a jacket, and I couldn't bend low enough to slip on socks, so Kess helped me dress. Though the fabric was soft, the waistband dug painfully into my sensitive skin.

Another friend of mine owned a car company in town and had offered to send a limousine to bring me home. The stretch Hummer picked up Thomas and the girls for the drive from the Upper Valley to Boston. The girls went crazy inside the luxury car, singing and dancing and hollering to a hip-hop CD they listened to five times.

Even without sight—or maybe even *more* without sight—I could feel how high their energy was when they came rushing into my room. The girls were hyped up, talking loudly and laughing with each other and Kess. I knew they were as excited as I was to be going home.

"Mom, you're a babe!" Liza exclaimed, seeing me in my new tracksuit.

"Oh, my God." I laughed, lifting my arms as high as I could in celebration. "We're going home."

They wheeled me outside to the car, and Kess gave me a hand as I stood from the chair. My steps were short and shuffling, and I held tightly to Kess's arm as I approached the Hummer. My family guided me: "Good. Almost there." Moving blindly filled me with a sense of fear and vulnerability that was entirely new. I had no choice but to trust the voices that were directing me and the gentle touches that kept me steady. Throughout, I clung to the belief that my blindness was temporary.

"Okay, here we are," Kess said. "Carm, feel the door. You'll have to step up to get into the car."

"Here," Thomas said. "Take my arm."

I took hold of Thomas, trying to figure out how to do this. The car was higher than I'd thought, and my knees didn't bend enough to take that big step. Anytime I tried, the skin felt as if it were cracking open. Just the light touch of my pants made me want to scream.

"Are you sure you want to do this, Carm?" Kess asked.

"There is no way I'm not going home," I managed. Tears fell as I turned around and forced my stiff legs into a squatting position. I eased my butt onto the step and, inch by inch, scooted in backwards. It took a full minute, but finally I slid exhaustedly into a seat. My family cheered as if I had won the Olympics.

It was two and a half hours from Boston to Thetford, and my stomach quickly rolled with nausea. But the girls and Kess were talking over each other, laughing and singing, so I leaned against Thomas and basked in everyone's joy. Between exhaustion and my medications, I soon fell asleep.

"Mom!" the girls said some time later. "Mom, we're home!"

The limo pulled up our driveway, and I shifted around to scoot out of the car backwards again. I managed it faster this time.

The November air was cold and brisk, and I breathed in deeply. I was so happy to be home and yet so disappointed that I couldn't see anything. The last time I had been here, my garden was just starting to grow. I imagined that it was all weeded out now, covered with a dusting of recent snow.

We walked through the garage, and Kess said, "Step. Step," as we neared the door. Haltingly, I took the two steps up. We walked into a small hallway, where the washer and dryer were hidden behind a set of accordion doors. There was a closet to the right and the pantry on our left. Then we walked into the kitchen. Right away, I could distinguish the voices of my mother, father, brothers, and sister-in-law. The house was warm and rich with the smell of ham, which Mom had put in the oven early that day.

"It smells good," Hannah's voice came from beside me. I could *feel* her happiness and relief. "It smells like home."

"Welcome back, Carm!" my mother said, coming up and hugging me gently.

I let Kess lead me into the living room, where I lowered myself into a chair and absorbed the positive energy around me. There was no heaviness in those moments. Herb was not there. As hard as I *knew* the road ahead would be, it felt as though something had been completed: the first six months were over.

Liza's voice came from beside me. "Thomas painted. Did you know?"

"I did. Kess mentioned it in rehab."

She had told me Thomas had helped with repairs on the house—the sliding glass door, painting the walls. I didn't understand at first why he'd painted. It was a new house, and the walls had always been white. Then I realized there must have been bloodstains. It was a gruesome thought—a house-turned-horror-movie.

"I was here before things were fixed," Liza said.

"I heard that, too. I wish you hadn't been."

When I had first gotten to the hospital, Kathie needed to find my living will. Liza didn't hesitate—she told her she knew where it was and would go with Kathie to get it. As always, she was teeming with curiosity and never repulsed, disgusted, or frightened. It reminded me of when a cat had died when she was little. I buried it before work as Liza stood over me, watching with her big brown eyes.

Her voice now was bubbling, eager, as if she'd been waiting ages for the opportunity to talk to me.

"It was so crazy, Mom. That night. Remember when Hannah got the knife? And then we went outside, and I don't know why we started throwing rocks against the window."

It was the first time we had talked about it, because when the girls came down to visit on Sundays, Kathie and Bill were always in the room. If I was ever alone with either Liza or Hannah, it wasn't for long. In retrospect, I wasn't fully ready to talk about it, but Liza was open, receptive. I felt as if she'd been waiting to get it off her chest, all these details of what she and Hannah had seen and done that night, and it didn't matter who was around; the doorbell kept ringing with friends and neighbors, but Liza never left her post beside me.

Hannah milled around, playing on the computer and talking to family and a few of her friends who stopped by. After a while, my mother let us know that the food was ready. She'd been preparing for hours, and we all gathered for ham, mashed potatoes, green beans, biscuits, and stuffing. It was Thanksgiving three days early, and we sat close together at the dining room table: my parents, Kess, the girls, and my brother, sister-in-law, and nephew. Kess fed me small forkfuls of food as everyone talked. I couldn't sit up for the whole meal and eventually excused myself to lie down.

"Girls, are you going to be okay?" I asked them.

"Yeah, Mom," Hannah said. "Kess's going to sleep with us."

"Okay," I said. "If there any problems, just come wake me, okay?"

"Okay, Mom."

After I'd said my goodnights, Kess walked me into the bedroom and helped me out of the tracksuit. As I carefully got into bed, I thought that if the girls and I could live there and accept that house as ours the way I thought it was, it would do more for our spirit and psychological wellbeing than anything else could. But I recognized that my blindness spared me in some ways. I didn't have to *see* the spot in the living room where I had first glimpsed Herb crouching; or my bedroom, where he had reached for the bat; or Liza's room, where I had flown headfirst into her dresser. The girls had to see all those places where they'd felt fear. They had to walk those same spots where they'd gotten glass in their feet from the broken door, twist the same lock on the bathroom door where they had sought shelter. I knew it was to our benefit to stay there, but I didn't want to get *my* power back at the detriment of the kids. All I could hope was that this was the next chapter and that it would all work out.

I woke the next morning clearly, sharply, with no disorientation. My first thought was, *How are the kids?* My mother, who had slept beside me, helped me up and into the kitchen. Kess was there already, drinking a cup of coffee.

"Was everything okay last night?" I asked.

"It was good," Kess said with a smile in her voice. "We had the air mattresses on the floor and spread out a bunch of blankets and pillows. It was a big slumber party. We fell asleep, and everybody was fine."

Relief washed over me. "That's so great."

From the stove, I heard the sound of eggs cracking and sizzling. My mom was making omelets as the girls padded into the kitchen.

"How're you girls doing?" I asked them over breakfast. "Was everything okay last night?"

"Yep," Liza said.

"Well, let me know if it's not, and we'll figure it out."

"Okay, Mom."

I was grateful that there wasn't a larger conversation about it. So many other things were so difficult that if something was going to be easy, I'd let it be easy. The first night was over. We had won.

∘ ∘ ∘

It's amazing how adaptable humans are, how quickly we can settle into realities that were once unimaginable. I probably went home earlier than I should have, which made things harder for everyone, but slowly, we found a rhythm.

In the beginning, Kess—who slept with me at night— woke me up at six in the morning. I took light hold of her elbow as she led me into the kitchen and made coffee. The smell transported me to normal mornings when I had woken up and set the Mr. Coffee to brew, never considering how lucky I was to see my daughters, to move without pain. I drank a little coffee, and my mother took the kids to school. Then I fell asleep again on the living room couch, propped up with pillows and blankets.

My dressing changes were every other day; there was no way I could tolerate them more often. Most of the time, they took two hours, start to finish. Undressing and stepping into the shower, trying to allow water onto my body and open wounds, was excruciating.

"Don't, Kess," I cried, when she tried to put soapy water on my head. "Please not today. I can't."

"Carm, I'm sorry." Her voice cracked. "We have to get these clean, though. Don't we?"

Some days I swallowed my pain, channeled my previous nurse-self and said yes, of course, we did. Other days I couldn't be strong. "Not today," I would say. "I just can't."

I knew dressing changes were always going to hurt. Kess felt she wasn't being gentle enough, not doing a good enough job. As consumed in my own pain as I was, I knew that the best thing I could do to ease my *family's* pain was to be the best patient I could. I wouldn't blame Kess for hurting me; that was just the nature of my wounds. I wouldn't bitch at my mother for being overly cautious, telling me there was a step where I *knew* there was a step; I was blind, and I was her daughter. I wouldn't snap at the girls for leaving their backpacks in the hallway; they were teenagers. Everyone was adjusting their lives to take care of me, and I had to respect that as much as I could.

Still, there were times the girls heard me cry from the bathroom. "What's wrong with Mom?" they'd ask, aghast.

Kess told them, "It's her head. The water hurts her the most there."

Though Kess had accepted the responsibility of helping me with the dressing changes, for which I'll always be grateful, working with the open wounds terrified her, and I was glad I didn't have to see it reflected in her eyes.

After the dressing changes, Kess and I shuffled back to the kitchen for breakfast. For a long time, my mother made me Quaker Oats Maple Brown Sugar Oatmeal or a cheese omelet. I had to be fed for the first few months because my hands didn't reach that high. The scar tissue on my neck was like tightly wound rows of rubber bands, and it pulled down one corner of my mouth; there was a space just large enough to slip a baby spoon into, and my mother fed me like an infant.

After breakfast—which was already early afternoon—I napped for three or four hours. I rose before dinner, when the kids returned from school. While Kess took me for a walk around the house for "exercise," I talked to the girls.

"Are you behaving in school?" I asked, thinking of Liza's rough years back in Hawthorne.

"Yes, Mom," they said. From the tone of their reply, I could imagine the rolls of their eyes.

"Mom, we want to stop going to therapy," Liza said. I'd been hearing the same whine since I woke up in September. Each Sunday, they'd begged me to let them stop going, but I insisted they continue until after I got home.

"But *why*?" Hannah asked. "You're home now. You said we could stop."

I could tell they were sick of it—*all* of it. They just wanted to let everything go and be normal kids again, and therapy reminded them of everything that had happened. I wouldn't make them continue it long-term, but the immediate value was undeniable. They needed to be able to process what had happened and the way all our lives had changed in a space where someone was there to listen only to them.

"Look, just do it a little bit longer," I said. "It's important for you, okay?"

After dinner, Mom or Kess read me sections from the newspaper, or we all sat in front of the television. I listened to the news or Jon Stewart or Jeopardy. Around eight, I went to bed, completely exhausted. The next day, the routine began again.

Depending on others to do everything for me was difficult because I had been so independent. At first, it was humiliating. It was as though I'd returned to toddlerhood or sped toward old age without even realizing it, and now I could do nothing for myself. What if I could never see again? I couldn't ask my family to give up their lives, their needs, indefinitely to take care of me. What would I do if nothing improved in a few years and they had to move on with their lives? It was overwhelming. The only way I could cope was to let go and let them do the best they could. The experience of total dependence taught me how to open up and truly receive—which may be a harder lesson than learning to give. I did all I could to be understanding, to remember the effort my family was putting in. I could only do that by verbally supporting them.

"I know it's hard," I said to Kess during dressing changes. I took a deep breath to steady my voice. "But I really appreciate all that you're doing. I know I cry, but it's not your fault. This, too, shall pass."

This, too, shall pass. I repeated the words often to myself.

At that point, Thomas worked three days a week at the hospital. When he wasn't working, he relieved Kess of the dressing changes. She rented a room in Hanover and worked on her psychology dissertation in her time off.

"If I lived here," he ventured, "I could do this for you all the time."

Just the mention of moving in together overwhelmed me. I was barely getting through daily life; I didn't have the emotional capacity to be a partner to him or anyone else. He may have been staying to "do the right thing," but ours wasn't a healthy relationship. How could it be?

Eventually, he started keeping things from me. Before I had gotten hurt, we'd talked about how Thomas needed to let his son suffer the consequences of his mistakes, but Thomas found that difficult. When his son and a friend moved in with him rent-free, he didn't tell me. It wasn't until I asked him point blank one day that he admitted they'd been staying with him for a while.

"You know you're not helping those kids," I said. "They're just using you."

"I know."

"And I can't handle you not being up front about little things like this. I already went through this with Herb."

"I'm sorry," Thomas said, his voice tense.

Neither of us said the obvious: this wasn't working. We continued with our routine—Thomas spending the night when Kess was gone, changing my dressings on days he didn't work, holding my hand, saying, "I love you." But I knew with absolute certainty that I didn't want a relationship. It wasn't fair to him. I had nothing to give—I could only take, and I didn't want to put myself in a position where I'd feel I had to make it up later. I allowed myself to get irritated with him to build up the strength to end things. He played a little game, for example, where he'd hold things in front of my face. I'd see a flash of light and ask what it was. He'd reply, "Oh, it's a soda can. I just wanted to see if you could see it." I let those little immature instances make me disproportionately angry.

One day, when Kess took over after several of Thomas's rounds, she gasped. "Oh, God, Carm," she said. "Something is wrong."

The fabric of her blouse brushed my cheek as she leaned in to look at my head. "What?"

"You have all these … pus pockets."

"Well, how many? Are they bad?"

She counted quietly under her breath, all the way up to twelve. "They're definitely infected."

It turned out to be a superficial infection called pseudomonas that a lot of people get in the hospital. I had been home for six weeks but was so injured that it was difficult to tell what my head wounds were "supposed" to look like versus when they were infected. Even as a nurse, I couldn't tell that I was feeling more pain than I was supposed to. I was in the hospital for three weeks while the infection was cleaned, and then I went in for another skin graft, where cadaver skin was placed on the surface of my open head wounds.

During that hospitalization, a therapist tried to teach me how to eat. It was hard to poke a piece of chicken with a fork when I couldn't see, and at one point the bowl kept spinning in a circle on my little tray. Thomas and the therapist started to laugh, and I broke with frustration and sadness.

"Get the fuck out!" I yelled, throwing the bowl. "Both of you! Get out!"

I wept in anger.

When the therapist returned, she told me they hadn't

been laughing at me. Maybe she was telling the truth, but it didn't matter at that point. The moment had served its purpose: I was more motivated than ever to feed myself. By the time I returned home, I was able to get food to my mouth with my hands. It wasn't comfortable and it wasn't pretty, but it was one tiny step closer to independence.

Thomas stayed with me at home for three days after I returned from the hospital. When Kess came back and did the first dressing change, she swore. "Carm, the infection is back."

"What? It's back? But Thomas was just here! He saw it twelve hours ago!"

"And he didn't say anything?"

"No."

"Well, this has been here for longer than twelve hours. We have to call the doctor again."

I was mutely livid. Thomas was a nursing assistant. He should have recognized it—and he must have. He just didn't want me to hurt anymore. He didn't want to tell me I needed to return to the hospital. It was the last straw.

I called him the next night, with Kess helping to hold the phone to my ear. "Thomas," I said, "I can't be in a relationship with you."

"What? What do you mean? Why not?"

"I just need my own space, my own time to try to get through this," I said. "I appreciate all you've done for me and the kids, and I don't want you to feel like you've done anything wrong ... but I'm not in any position to maintain a relationship—with you or anyone else."

I could hear him breathing hard on the other line. "I think you just need to think about it a little longer. I don't think this is the best thing. Carmen, I don't know what

I'd do without you."

What *he'd* do without *me?* Was he kidding? I was giving him the chance to walk away. He should have run. He should have said thank you.

It was a long conversation, and I cried and apologized and reiterated that I couldn't have a relationship. "I don't know when I'll be able to have sex again, and I'm not going to have you waiting for me. I'm letting you off the hook—why don't you just take it?"

I never told him I was upset about the dressing changes. He had tried; how could I hold that against him?

○ ○ ○

Months passed before I drew the courage to walk into Liza's room. That was where Herb had done the most damage to me, but I thought, *Liza's been in here. She's okay with it. I can be okay with it, too.*

When I stepped through the doorframe, it was with a heavy, intense awareness. My body prickled. I remembered my head bashing into her bureau drawers and the helplessness of having my hands tied behind my back. I made myself stand there for as long as I could before retreating.

For much of that first year, I went through what happened a million times in my head. I changed small details that meant I didn't get hurt. I listened to the little voice that urged, "Call him for his birthday." I imagined him picking up the phone, hearing my voice wishing him well, and turning his truck around. Other times, I remembered that we had a couple of child-sized baseball bats, and one was leaned up against the corner of the bedroom; what if I had walked out of the room with the bat in my hand?

He was squatted down and wouldn't have expected me to have a weapon; I could have crushed his skull. Or what if I hadn't been so groggy? I could have reacted more quickly, run back into the room for the bat, defended myself better. Or—I'd had conversations with Thomas about whether I should buy a gun for protection, now that I was a single mother again. But I was in Thetford, not LA, and didn't want a gun around my kids anyway. Thomas said, "Well, maybe not a real gun, but how about a Taser?" I asked him if they were legal, and he said he didn't know. What if I had done more research? What if I had bought one anyway? I could have Tasered Herb and rushed the girls out of the house, and no one would have gotten hurt but him. Sometimes I lost myself in these scenarios so completely that I was startled to no longer perceive light beyond my eyelids; the room had darkened around me without my even noticing, and I had no idea how long I had chased these thoughts around my mind.

Every time I startled away from those alternate pasts, I tried to reason with myself: if any one of those "what ifs" had happened, he wouldn't be in jail. He would be after me again and again, and then what would I do? I wouldn't be able to live in Thetford and have a good life. I'd always be on the run, worried that he would hurt me or someone else. So, even though I was still so injured, with such a long road ahead, I had a sense of relief: he was in jail. I didn't need to be afraid of loud noises or unexpected knocks on the door; he couldn't hurt us anymore. And that was something.

CHAPTER 11

A
WORLD
DIMMED

SIX OR EIGHT MONTHS BEFORE I GOT HURT, HANNAH had randomly asked, "Mom, if you had a choice, would you rather be blind or deaf?" She was sitting on the living room couch, and I was cleaning. I didn't even have to think about my answer: "Deaf, of course. No one wants to be blind!"

I wasn't taken aback by Hannah's question, because it was so normal and kid-like. I never actually *considered* being blind; it was one of those monumental, irreconcilable things one never thinks will happen to them. And that's okay, because worrying about what we can't control is wasted energy. Looking back, however, that moment says to me that there were experiences coming my way that my youngest daughter could somehow intuit. It leads me to believe there are some parts of life—very few—that are scripted, meant to happen at a specific time for a specific reason, and all the choices in the world will lead to the same place. In my case, that was blindness.

My corneas were so damaged that I wouldn't be able to see even if my eyes were open. Among all my injuries, this was the most confounding. The world was dark to me,

129

endless velvet blackness that only sometimes brightened against my sewn skin. I was consumed with questions. When could I have surgery? Did they really think they could replace my corneas? How much would I be able to see? Would I be able to drive again? How was I going to work? What would I do if I could no longer be a nurse? I countered my terror of not being able to see again by reminding myself, "Carm, blind people live alone all the time. Even if you never regain sight, you won't always be this dependent." It was my only saving grace.

Though I couldn't accept the prospect of being blind forever, I *did* need to accept my immediate reality: I couldn't see, so I had to take people at their word. I no longer had visual cues—crossed arms, an averted gaze, blushing—to gauge if people were lying, so it was either trust everyone or trust no one. There were times I could tell when someone was not necessarily telling the truth, like when I asked my mother or sister to describe me, and they said I was me "but with scars." They weren't being entirely honest, I sensed, but what was the point in pressing the issue? Life gives you what you need, and life took my sight so I wouldn't have to immediately deal with my disfigurement. Plus, calling out mistruths didn't seem important anymore. If people wanted me to know something, they would tell me; if they lied, that was on them. I was learning to read people and situations, but I was not interested in going on truth-seeking investigations. It was all I could do to deal with my immediate physical realities.

In the early days, an occupational therapist was sent to my house to work with me. I sat in a chair near the doorway, working with bungee cords to stretch my stiff arms. When we were done, I asked, "Can I get up now?"

"Yes, we're all through," the occupational therapist said.

I struggled up from the chair and walked straight into a wall.

Aside from the pain, the sensation of bumping into walls is completely jarring. It was bad enough doing it by myself, but as a nurse, I was upset by the therapist's carelessness; she was standing right in front of me and overlooked my going in the wrong direction. As a result, I developed a bump on my head that would take a year to heal.

The occupational therapist never returned.

Over time, my family and I created our own little ways of adapting to blindness. Once I was able to feed myself, Kess or my mother described the food on my plate by using the clock.

"You've got green beans at twelve," Kess said, "mashed potatoes at three, and chicken at seven."

"Thank you," I said. Knowing where my food was gave me the dignity of intentionality; I wasn't just haphazardly stabbing my fork toward the plate, learning what I was eating only when it was in my mouth.

Kess and I also mastered a tandem walk. In narrow or crowded places, like a hospital lobby, I stood half a step behind her with one hand on her shoulder. She bent one arm back, and I used my other hand to hold hers. I followed the rhythm of her steps as though we were partners on a dance floor. She narrated our path as we moved: "One step up; okay, step down; ramp." With Kess's guidance, I didn't need my cane and preferred not to use it anyway.

At home, if it was cold outside, Kess walked me around the house for exercise. If it was warmer, we walked outdoors in the morning and then later at night. Sometimes, I stood still in the kitchen for three or four minutes, as long as I could bear before the nerve damage in my legs grew too painful.

Mostly, though, I lived a sedentary life. My dressing drained me, so I spent most of my time sitting in the middle of the living room sofa, pillows and blankets making small hills around me.

With all its limitations, being blind opened up a whole other world within that is hard to access when all you see is the material world. My sense of hearing, even with one ear, was the first to heighten. When I lay in bed during a light rain, the sound of water falling on the roof was so loud and clear that it was as if it were raining on my shoulder. I also learned how much we rely on our vision at the sacrifice of simple intuition. With sight, how many times had I dropped a pill on the floor and spent minutes on my hands and knees, straining to see where it must have rolled under a hospital bed or behind a trashcan? Now, when I dropped something, if I bent down and reached out my hand, nine out of ten times the object was right there. It was as if my body took over for me, leading me to what I needed.

Once I made that realization, I praised my body constantly. "I have the strongest body in the world," I'd say. Even though I had been a tomboy before, largely unconcerned with how my hair looked or whether I was thin enough, I had never appreciated how *strong* my body could be if I wanted it to. People say that if the attack had happened five years earlier and technology weren't what it was in 2007, I might not have survived. That may be true, but I also think we don't know how powerful our bodies are when we want to live. My survival was more than scientific advancement; it was will. It was choice.

Being blind also changed how I mothered Liza and Hannah. They were fifteen and thirteen, and I wondered how I would discipline them if I couldn't see. My mother and sister didn't want to cross those parental lines—nor did I want them to—so I would need to burden the girls with something heavy: trust.

"Listen," I said to them. "You know I can't see, so when I ask you to do something, you need to just do it. When something is going on at school or in your personal lives, you need to tell me about it. And know that I am still going to discipline you if something goes wrong. I'm still your mother first. Got it?"

"Yes, Mom," they said, and I heard in their grumbling tones a relieved sense of normalcy.

In the first week of February 2008, the girls finally got what they'd been whining for since September: to cease therapy. The therapist didn't want them to stop going, and I knew she had the girls' best interests at heart, but no one knew my daughters better than I did. If I forced them to continue therapy for any longer, they were not going to get anything out of it. If their grades dropped, I would put them back in; otherwise, I felt they were well adjusted enough to move on. Our lives are a series of choices, and I respected theirs.

While the girls stopped going to therapy, I continued. I knew it was a necessity and encouraged all my family members to go, too. Kess had gone while I was in my coma—she was a psychology doctoral candidate and had connections in the area—but afterwards, she and my mother argued that insurance wouldn't cover it and they couldn't afford therapy out of pocket.

"I'll pay for it," I said. "It's important."

Recovery was going to be a joint effort. Everyone was as hurt and troubled as I was. My mother and sister were incredible caregivers, holding themselves together in front of me, but it didn't mean they weren't overwhelmed with the enormity of our life changes.

No one took me up on my offer. Even Kathie, the loudest advocate for therapy while I was in rehab, never went to see anyone herself. Why? I didn't know. It was as if everyone was so focused on helping me that they didn't think about helping themselves. That wasn't good for anyone. Again, though, those were their choices.

Every Monday at eleven o'clock, my mother drove me to therapy at Hitchcock. I was nervous the first time, but my therapist simply introduced herself and told me what she knew of my story. Fairly quickly, I was at ease.

Therapy felt like one long day; each session, I walked in and my therapist asked, "How are you doing today?" I never knew until I sat down what the answer was. Then I decided that the best thing I could do was be honest, whatever it was. Therapy became one of my only outlets. I didn't hold back with my therapist the way I did with my mother, sister, or Kathie. She wasn't family or a friend, and I could say what I wanted to without burdening anyone with more stress than they already had. I gave the heaviness of my fears and heartbreak to my therapist, and she accepted them. That release was exactly what I needed at the time. I needed to be able to cry about my eyesight, what I looked like, and all the challenges I was trying to face without worrying about how it was affecting my listener.

I was most depressed that summer. In May, Dr. Samir Melki of Boston Laser had told me I was ready to have a synthetic corneal transplant on my left eye. It was a novel and rarely used procedure, meant for people unable to accept cadaver corneas. Though I could accept a regular organ transplant, the lye Herb had poured on me would dissolve a human cornea. Synthetic corneas were my only hope for sight. However, Dr. Melki couldn't get me on his schedule until July. I went through a terrible crying spell that lasted for days because I couldn't imagine waiting another eight weeks. With everything else I was dealing with, I knew it was almost ridiculous to take this so hard, but I couldn't help it. I cried and cried, making myself sick, until finally I was prescribed Zoloft. The antidepressant numbed me enough that I didn't always feel so cracked open and raw.

There were some days, sitting before my therapist, that I wasn't miserable. I was optimistic and joyful and strong. I talked about all the ways I thought things would be okay: that, one way or another, I had lessons to learn; and one way or another, I was going to find my happiness again. It was all attitude.

No matter what kind of day I had, I felt better as soon as I walked out, as if I'd let my core, unfiltered feelings go. I could get back into the car and think, *That's over. I don't need to do that anymore today.* I could go home to my kids and mom and sister and know they didn't have to deal with it. Then I could look forward again.

CHAPTER 12

VIEWER DISCRETION

IN JULY, FINALLY, DR. MELKI PERFORMED MY FIRST synthetic cornea transplant. The surgery took about an hour, and he removed the damaged central part of my cornea and replaced it with the synthetic one. For the next month, I waited anxiously to return to his office for what I thought would be the great reveal: he was opening my eye, which had been stitched shut again after surgery.

Dr. Melki was soft-spoken and kind. "Okay, Carmen," he said gently. "I've opened your eye a bit. Tell me what you can see."

I had thought that my field of vision would be wide and sprawling, even if the images were still blurry. I didn't realize how tiny the hole I'd be peering through would be; it was like trying to see the whole sky through an aperture the size of a pea.

"Not much," I said uncertainly. "Not much at all. It's going to get better, right?"

"It should," Dr. Melki said. "Let's go ahead and clean it out, and we'll set up a follow-up appointment."

For the next few minutes, Dr. Melki rid my eye of its mucus and drainage, explaining how to do this at home. Then we made an appointment for a few weeks later.

It was that afternoon, while sitting on the toilet, of all

places, that I cast my eye downward and saw something I hadn't seen in a year: color! I could make out the cheerful pop of my bright magenta tank top. It was the most beautiful thing I'd ever seen.

"I can see the color of my tank top!" I said to my family, excited. "Isn't that great? I'm sure it'll just get better from here!"

While I waited to see improvement, I decided to focus my energy on something else—something positive.

When I was in rehab and Kess was still updating my CarePages website, she told me that people all over the country were following my story. Some wrote letters and sent cards, and others held fundraisers and donated money. The word *inspiration* was used a lot. One woman who worked with domestic violence victims talked about my attack at a meeting one night. Apparently, Kess told me, it prompted a dozen women to leave their abusive husbands. I was startled that my story could have such power, but it made me feel good. Somehow, as injured as I was, I had helped people. Telling my story could help people.

It was August of 2008, and I was still receiving a steady stream of visitors at home. Kess told me of the way I talked to them, "You're so open. What you said just flowed. I'm amazed that you can talk like that."

"You know what?" I said. "I'm amazed, too. But I think this is what I need to do because no one does it."

As a nurse, I had seen so many people overcome and silenced by the pain they suffered—the shame of domestic violence, the guilt of addiction, the burden of hate—and I didn't want to be silenced by what Herb had done. I didn't want to hide. After my conversation with Kess, I thought, *This is something I can do. I can talk. I can let people know I am okay. I can let others like me know they don't have to hide.*

Kess had been keeping track of the names and phone numbers of reporters who had written about me, and I asked her to contact John Curran. John (who, sadly, passed away in 2011) worked for the Associated Press and had written a piece about me while I was in my coma. He had also emailed Kess after the *Valley News* published a piece on my synthetic cornea transplant. His was the only name that stuck in my mind, and I figured his reach with the Associated Press might be wider than that of someone at a specific publication. I asked Kess to email him back.

"Okay, Carm," she said. "If that's what you want."

My family never inhibited anything I wanted to do. Though they are private people, they supported my choice to reach out with my story.

My phone rang not long after. When he gave me his name, I said, "I'd like to be interviewed."

"Oh," he said, as if taken aback. "Well, sure. I can go to your house. Would it be okay if I bring a photographer?"

"That's fine."

We set up a time within the week. While I waited for the day to arrive, I thought constantly about having my picture taken. It was the first time since I'd been hurt that my photo would be captured, and though I knew I wouldn't see it, I was nervous. I wanted to look the best I could, under the circumstances, but I wasn't going to cover up my scars. It was summer, and the scars on my neck and chest were so thick I couldn't sweat. So, that day, I wore a tank top despite knowing the scars would be overwhelming to look at.

In the early afternoon, my most comfortable time of day, John and his photographer came to my door. I could tell by the photographer's voice that he was young. John, I knew, was about ten years older than I was. He was a seasoned reporter.

Kess and Mom were at the house, and we stayed in the living room for the interview. The girls were teenagers and didn't want their pictures taken, so they stayed in their room. I sat on the couch I had spent much of the last year on—a three-seater, where I occupied the middle.

"I'm going to set up over here," the photographer said. His youthful voice was sweet and polite. "If anything makes you uncomfortable, just let me know."

"Thank you." I was touched by his consideration.

Though John had been doing this for years, I sensed quickly that he was nervous. His voice was hesitant, and he stumbled with his questions. I couldn't help but take it personally; was I *that* hard to be around?

"What do you see when you look in the mirror?" he asked at one point.

"I don't see anything in the mirror," I said, somewhat snarkily. "I'm blind."

"Oh, yeah, right. Of course."

The hell with it if he's uncomfortable, I thought. I couldn't worry about how he was coping with being around me. It helped that I couldn't see his look of unease, and I realized I could use that to my advantage. I had to use everything I could, because if I could do this—be public with my story—there was a chance I could help people.

"I can see certain colors now, but that's all," I said, softening. "I'm hoping to see a lot more soon."

"And how are your kids doing?"

"They're good. Their grades haven't dropped, and they're happy."

Though it was just my first interview, I knew I would never discuss the girls in the media beyond the basics. I also wasn't going to tell anybody what had happened that night—at least not in detail. If John had asked whether I wanted to talk about it, I would have said, "No. I'm not going there." At the time, it didn't feel right. The attack was gruesome and gross; it wasn't what people needed to know right then. There wasn't any good to make of it yet.

On September 8, 2008, John Curran's article was published. The paper was delivered to my house, and Mom went outside to grab it. When she came back, she spread the paper before her and read the piece to me out loud. I listened to John's writing and my own words. Did it feel okay to share my story? There was so much I hadn't said; would I want to do this again? *Could* good come from it?

"He did a good job," I said, when Mom had finished reading. "I like it."

"I like it, too," Mom said.

In the next few days and weeks, Mom and Kess heard from dozens of people who read the article. They said how happy they were that I was doing okay. They called me "brave." I didn't see it that way—I was still just surviving—but the positive feedback made a difference to me in those difficult days. It gave me hope that things could get better.

° ° °

The next month was Herb's suppression hearing to evaluate whether his Miranda rights had been violated. If so, several statements he made that night (I didn't know which ones) would get tossed out. I would be called to answer general questions about his intelligence, through which the state prosecutor would try to prove that Herb was lucid enough to understand his rights. The prosecutor hadn't told Herb's defense attorney I would be there. Herb had no idea he was going to see me.

On the Thursday morning of the hearing, Mom, Kess, and I drove to court together. I was buzzing with nerves; it would be the first time I was in the same room with Herb since the attack. The air in the car pulsed with our shared anxiety. I focused all my energy on fighting motion sickness, which is so much worse when you're blind. I couldn't wait until the day was done.

Another hearing was under way when we arrived, so the prosecutor showed us into a separate waiting room. Immediately, I sank into a large chair. This was my first real outing, except for my trips to the hospital in Boston, since I'd been hurt. I was already painfully exhausted.

"Is there a place in court I can sit where he'll walk near me?" I asked Kess as we waited. "I want him to get a good look at what he did."

I was heavily bandaged, still with open wounds and healing skin grafts.

"The front row," she said.

Before long, a court employee escorted us out of the room. I held Kess's arm, and with our slow, practiced shuffle, we walked to the front of the courtroom. I followed her into a row, sitting on the aisle. Herb would have to walk right past me on the way to his seat.

"Squeeze my hand when he's coming," I whispered to Kess.

Even to my heightened sense of hearing, the room was stark silent. Then doors opened, and I heard the metallic clank of chains. Kess squeezed my hand constantly, compulsively. Her breathing changed as she started crying. Slow, measured footsteps approached, along with that heavy clanking.

"It's okay," I said out loud. "It's okay. Don't worry."

The chains got within a few feet of me and paused. Automatically, I began to rise. My hands were fisted at my sides, nails digging into my palms. Herb looked, I was told later, as though he were going to walk straight up to me. He was staring—couldn't take his eyes off me. His face was crinkled, as if he had a hard time looking at the bandaged and blind woman who used to be his wife. Then a sheriff's deputy stepped between us, and another deputy gripped Herb's arm and guided him to his chair.

As the hearing started, I was hyperaware of Herb's presence. It was eerie to know he was right in front of me, chained at the waist and ankles, when I couldn't see him. I felt as if I were in a dream: I could hear everything and knew what was happening, but I had to visually create the scene in my mind. I imagined the judge sitting stoically in the front of the room. I imagined Herb's handcuffed wrists resting on the table, his attorney taking notes on a legal pad beside him. I imagined reporters in the back, scribbling in shorthand, and my family looking at the man who had caused so much pain.

The hearing lasted a few hours. I listened to all the evidence the police related, and then Kess helped me up to the stand. Not being able to see Herb probably made my time up there easier.

The prosecutor asked me the questions I expected: how

Herb and I had met; when we had married; and whether we had lived together before being married.

"We did," I said, fighting tears.

"For how long?"

"Two and a half years … almost three."

"Did you buy a house together in California?"

"We did."

"Did you buy a house together in Vermont?"

"We did."

"Did he suffer from any mental illness that you knew of?"

I hesitated. *Look at me now!* I thought. "Not that I know of, no."

After a few minutes, the prosecutor said to Kess, "You can help her down now."

After the hearing, a woman approached me outside the courthouse.

"My name is Jennifer Hauck," she said. "I'm with the *Valley News.* How are you feeling right now?"

"I'm happy it's over," I said. "I'm ready to go home."

"I can imagine." The sympathy in her voice sounded sincere. "Well, I won't keep you long. I just wanted to ask—we would love to do a long series on your story, documenting your recovery in photographs. Would you be interested in working with us?"

I thought about it. My first media experience had been positive. Though I was still self-conscious about pictures, I said, "Give me a call. We can talk about it."

Back in the car with Mom and Kess, the energy felt different than it had that morning. Lighter. I had been in the same room as Herb and come out okay. I had spoken clearly on the stand. I hadn't broken down. I felt accomplished. This was one step closer to seeing him in jail.

It was early afternoon when we got home. We were all tired but excited for the news coverage of the hearing. The girls joined us in the living room, and I took my seat on the couch. When it hit five o'clock, we quieted as the news began.

"Warning," came a voice from the TV. "These images are graphic and may be disturbing to some viewers. Viewer discretion is advised."

My heart dropped.

"Oh, my God!" I said. "They're talking about me! They're talking about *me*?"

No one responded.

Graphic warning ... I had heard that before surgery shows—images of open wounds, blood. But I'd never heard it refer to a *person*. What did this mean? What did I *look* like?

I touched my face. My skin felt bumpy, and my fingers traced scars and broken areas, but I had two eyes. A nose. A bottom lip. I was missing an ear, but it wasn't as if half my face was gone. I couldn't conjure a mental image of myself or envision how I could look bad enough to warrant a *warning*. At the same time, it bothered me that society felt it *needed* to put a warning. So what if I didn't look pretty? If I didn't look normal? This was a person they were talking about!

After the news segment, which everyone said they liked, we watched our normal shows before I went to bed around eight. In those days, I never thought far beyond the moment because I just couldn't, but I knew that I would eventually need to deal with my disfigurement. A part of me was scared. Maybe it would be better if my sight never returned, so I never needed to see what I looked like. But that would just be another form of hiding.

The next day, I decided to ask Kess and Mom what I looked like. I approached them separately, Kess first.

"Kess?" I asked. We were both in the living room. "What do I look like? Can you describe it?"

Kess was silent for a moment. "Well," she sighed. "I just don't know how to say it, Carm. You're scarred—I don't know. I just really don't know."

Mom was even less helpful. "I can't put it into words," she said. "I can't help you with that. Sorry."

Oh God, I thought.

"Well," I said to Kess, frustrated, "at least I don't have to dress up for Halloween."

"What do you mean?" Kess asked.

"I can go as an accident victim."

"Carmen, that is not funny," Kess snapped.

"Sorry," I said sullenly.

My heart sank. How could I have not known things were this bad? Kess couldn't laugh at a stupid joke. My own mother couldn't describe me. They had *warned people about me* on TV. What was I supposed to do from now on, wear a warning on my chest so everybody would know I was coming? How could I move forward with everything I wanted to do if the world needed viewer discretion to look at me?

CHAPTER 13

VANQUISHING THE ENEMY

AFTER I HEARD THE GRAPHIC WARNING announcement on TV, what I refer to as my Disfigurement Challenge began.

During my Disfigurement Challenge, I was acutely concerned with how bad I must look. As it would happen, that negative energy kept reflecting back at me. One afternoon, Kess and I were on the bus heading into Boston for one of my doctor's appointments. The trip was several hours long, so Kess led me down the narrow aisle between seats to the bathroom near the back. The bus was loud with passengers talking, traffic outside, and wind pressing against the windows, but I was able to make out the distinct sound of crying.

"Daddy, Daddy, make him go away," whimpered a little girl. "He's scaring me."

As with the graphic warning, I halted with a belated, hard jolt of recognition. She was talking about *me*.

"No, it's okay, honey," I said, craning my head in the direction I thought her voice had come from. "You don't have to be scared. I'm a mommy."

"Carm," Kess said gently, touching my arm, "she can't

hear you."

"What do you mean?"

"Her dad took her to another seat."

I swallowed past the lump in my throat and went to use the restroom. Back at my seat, I couldn't hold back the tears. I was like a nut cracked wide open, completely unable to filter my emotions. "Jesus," I said. "Now I'm scaring little kids?" The unasked question was *How bad do I look?*

I spent the rest of that dark bus trip in silence, introspective about my situation. I had recently had three big surgeries in one week to place large skin grafts over the open wounds on my head. Dr. Bodham Pomahac, a plastic surgeon at Brigham in Boston, had taken skin from my legs, upper arm, and lower back to cover the open areas. The skin taken from my lower back was the size of a square napkin; it was undamaged by the lye because that was where my hands were tied. He grafted that skin to my head, which left a raw patch on my back where the surface skin was now gone. They covered the new wound with a yellow piece of gauze called Xeroform with a non-adherent petrolatum blend that helped prevent infection. When the gauze dried, it needed to be cut off to allow the new skin to grow.

After the surgery, Dr. Pomahac told Kess, "She's going to hate me for this because I took such a big piece. It's not going to heal in seven to ten days like the little pieces." He was right. It took weeks to heal. The wound kept opening and infecting, and Kess tried to attach pads to my waist to catch the drainage. My clothes stuck to the wound and hurt like hell to pull off, and I did hate Dr. Pomahac for it.

"Don't you ever take a piece this size again," I told him. "I can't do it. Never again."

Because the recovery was so difficult, I lost a lot of weight during that time. Once I reached a hundred pounds, I stopped weighing myself. *No wonder I scared that little girl*, I thought on the bus. I was not only ugly, not only a walking open wound, but also skeletal. I hated the thought of what I must look like.

○ ○ ○

Shortly after Herb's suppression hearing, the photographer from the *Valley News* called me. She wanted to talk to me about the piece they were proposing.

"Why don't you come over so we can talk in person?" I suggested.

We set up a day, and she knocked on the door as scheduled. Mom walked her into the living room, where I was sitting on the couch.

"Hi, Carmen," Jen said, her voice upbeat. "How are you feeling?"

"I'm all right," I said. "I'm getting by."

"That's *good*. That's really good."

Jen's warmth felt sincere. I sensed that I could trust her, and I liked her from the start.

We chatted for a few minutes, and then Jen said brightly, "So! What questions do you have for me?"

"Well," I said, "you said this is going to be a long article?"

"I'm not exactly sure," she said. "I want to take pictures of you for about a year. It'll depend on what you're doing, of course, but I'd go with you to doctors' visits, court hearings, and any other significant events."

"So the whole thing will be in pictures?"

"No, there'll be a written component as well. One of our reporters will come along when I go places with you. He'll just take notes and then maybe ask you some questions afterward. Does this sound like something you'd be interested in doing?"

My mind flashed to the little girl crying on the bus. Disfigurement Challenge or not, shying away from cameras wouldn't change how I looked. Besides, my photo had already been in the paper because of the Associated Press article. A lot could change in a year, and if I wanted to share my story, I had to get over—or at least ignore—my self-consciousness.

"I'd like to do it," I told Jen. "I just need to talk to my family and make sure they're okay with it."

"Of course," Jen said. "Take your time, and let me know what you decide."

After she left, I gathered my mom, Kess, and the girls together. "I know it's uncomfortable to be in the media," I said, "but so few people who go through things like this are willing to come forward. I want to do something different, and it's right here staring at me. It seems so obvious."

It also made me feel as if I were giving back to all the people who were giving to me. People had given me a lot—food, money, clothes, visits, cards—and I wanted to let them know their support meant something to me.

"I don't really know what this will entail," I said, "but I like Jen. Do you guys like her?"

My mom and Kess agreed they did.

"Well, then, I say we do this. If we don't like it or something goes wrong, we can always just end it. What do you all think?"

"I don't want my picture taken," my mother said instantly. That didn't surprise me. Though my mom's picture had been taken with me at court for the suppression hearing, she was leery of the media.

"Okay," I said. "I'll talk to Jen about that. What about the rest of you?"

"If this is what you want to do, Carm …," Kess said.

"Girls?" I asked.

"I don't care if they take my picture, but I don't want to have to talk to anyone," Liza said.

"Same for me," said Hannah.

"All right, then," I said. "I'll call Jen and say yes!"

∘ ∘ ∘

Jen was over at the house a lot that winter. She wanted to take real, candid photos, so she never told me when she was taking them. That's how I wanted it. I wanted her to capture what she could capture and do it the way she wanted to do it. Later on, when I was comfortable enough to move some small furniture in the living room, she said, "I'm not going to help you. I'm sorry, but I want to take pictures." I said that was fine; this was what I was going to be doing regardless of whether she was there.

Sometime before Christmas, I asked Jen when her birthday was. I felt so comfortable with her that—as into astrology as I was—I wanted to know her sign.

Jen hesitated. "I don't know if I should tell you."

"Why?"

"Well … it's June 9."

"Oh," I said. "That's Herb's birthday."

"I know," she said, almost apologetically. "I heard that in the courtroom."

"Where were you born?"

"Camden, New Jersey."

"Are you kidding me?" I said. "That's where Herb was born!"

"Oh, my God," Jen said. After a beat, she added, "That's a little creepy."

We were quiet for a few moments. Same birth date and place? What were the odds? I didn't believe in coincidence, but if there were meaning in it, I didn't know what it was.

I didn't meet Mark, the writer, until after Christmas. In his mid-twenties, Mark was sweet, polite, and, according to the girls, "super good-looking." He had wavy caramel-colored hair and blue eyes. He wasn't as experienced as the Associated Press reporter, John Curran, but then, John Curran hadn't been experienced in interviewing someone like me. For a young guy, Mark impressed me with his attentiveness and maturity. I felt as though he were more comfortable being uncomfortable, and that made me trust him.

He and Jen accompanied me to Boston several times over the next couple of months. By then, I was used to the continuous clicking of Jen's camera; sometimes I didn't even hear it, and I forgot they were there. She and Mark were both comfortable to be around. They fought like brother and sister sometimes, and my family teased them about their bickering.

I was so constantly surrounded by people that the first afternoon I spent alone was a major milestone. Liza had just turned sixteen, so she and Hannah were going to get some cash at the ATM and drive down to the outdoor mall in West Lebanon. It was the first time Liza had been able to drive her sister without another adult in the car, and I wanted them to have that experience.

"Are you sure you're going to be okay?" Liza asked.

"Yeah, we can stay until Gram or someone is here," Hannah added.

"No, I want you guys to go," I said. "I can be alone for a couple of hours—no problem."

They kissed me goodbye, and the moment was bittersweet. More than anything, I wished I could see my two girls walk out into the sunshine, laughing together as they slid into Liza's little Hyundai Elantra. I imagined Liza adjusting her rearview mirror, arranging her sunglasses over her eyes as Hannah turned the radio up. I envisioned how I'd wave as they reversed out of the long driveway and into the road. My girls were growing up.

Shortly after they left, there was a knock on the door. Nobody ever knocked; for that matter, no one ever came over unannounced. Everyone in Thetford knew me. They knew I was blind and that they needed to take extra considerations.

"Hello?" I called. I couldn't tell whether the knock was coming from the front door or garage door. Nobody answered. Footsteps rustled outside. "Hello?"

I was standing in the living room, between the kitchen and front door, straining to catch the sound of a voice. When I heard the knob turn, my heart thrashed in my chest. I froze as the front door eased open.

"Who is it?" I called in panic.

A male voice I didn't recognize said something like, "Sandy Cook."

I staggered my way to the couch, patting my hands around to search for the telephone. My fingers wrapped around it, and I dialed Liza's familiar number.

"Someone just came into the house!" I managed, my voice high and shaky. "I don't know who it was, he just came in. He didn't say anything. I don't know who it is."

"Okay, Mom, we're turning around," Liza said. "We're not even on the interstate yet, we'll be right there."

I was in tears, shaking. I knew no one was in the house anymore, but the residual terror remained as I waited for the girls to get home.

"Mom," Liza called as they burst through the door. "We're here, are you okay? What happened?"

"I don't know who it was," I said, crying. "I yelled out, but he never answered."

"It's okay, you're okay," Liza assured me.

It took about thirty seconds for the girls to see a box of candy resting by the front door.

"Mom, it's the candy," Hannah said. "Remember, Gram ordered it a few months ago?"

It was called *sandy* something. "Oh, my god," I said, weak as my rush of fear turned to relief and embarrassment. I collapsed onto the couch, a hand over my heart.

"We'll just stay here this afternoon," Liza said.

"No, no," I said. "You girls go. I can do this. Really. I'll be all right now."

I saw in that moment that there was no point in being afraid. I wanted to be independent. I wanted my kids to go shopping. I wanted to eventually live alone, like the normal adult woman I used to be. That goal pushed me forward.

I stayed by myself every chance I could after that. I asked my mother to start coming at ten in the morning instead of eight and looked forward to afternoons when the house would be empty. Kess still stayed with me at times, but she was already renting an apartment and transitioning out. Though I still couldn't help being *startled* by noises I wasn't expecting or didn't recognize, I never again felt the same terror I did that first afternoon. After all, I realized, I had already experienced the worst thing that could happen to me, and I had lived; what did I have left to fear?

CHAPTER 14

JUSTICE

BY FEBRUARY OF 2009, I HAD STARTED TO FEEL good in my mind. That month was Herb's sentencing. I could withstand any physical ailment as long as I knew that soon he would be behind bars for good; I'd no longer need to worry about him getting released on a technicality, or about going to more hearings, or about dragging the kids through additional court proceedings. I reveled in the refreshing sense of positivity.

The prosecutor and I had gone back and forth over the holidays, coming to settlement terms. Herb was being charged for maiming. This particular charge had nothing to do with disfigurement; it was all about blinding someone through violence. In Vermont, it carried the toughest punishment—thirty years without parole. The sentencing was just a formality; Herb didn't want a trial, so his future was sealed.

Since going to court was a physical hardship for me, the judge had agreed to hold the hearing on one date, instead of spread out across several. We would be in court for about three hours, which would still be a challenge, but it would be over after that day.

I talked to the girls beforehand. "I know you don't want to go," I said, "but I think it's in our best interest if we all go together. We're going to put this to rest. Kess will pick you guys up from school when it's time."

"No," Liza said. "We'll meet you at the top of the hill. I'll get Hannah and we'll follow you. Then we'll just drive back to school afterwards."

I instantly understood that they wanted the day to be as normal as possible. They liked going to school. It was where they could be themselves, letting their school life be their school life, unaffected by what had happened.

"That's fine with me," I said. "Kess will call you when we're leaving the driveway."

When the day came, the atmosphere was less stressful than that of the suppression hearing. We weren't walking into the unknown. We had already been to court. I had already faced Herb, so to speak; I had stood in the same room as him, taken the stand, let him see how badly he'd hurt me and yet that I was still alive.

"Bye, Mom!" Liza and Hannah called that morning. It was seven a.m., and they were heading to school.

"Bye!" I called back. "Remember, we need to be at court at nine. Kess will call you when it's time to leave."

"Yeah, we got it."

I smiled as their footsteps clattered toward the door. I imagined them shrugging on heavy winter coats and grabbing their backpacks. Liza's keys jangled, and again I felt a quick rush of surprise: Liza was sixteen, driving. Not a child anymore. The front door opened and closed, and an engine gunned to life in the driveway. A few seconds later, the vehicle noise was gone.

I breathed deeply to still what nerves were there. It was going to be a long day, and I would need to take the stand again, but I was ready for it. After all the unending surgeries and dressing changes in the last year and a half, I wanted at least one sense of completion: Herb attacked me, he was arrested, he was sentenced, and he went to jail. Completion.

I also knew this was going to be the last time he saw me. At the suppression hearing, I was bandaged up; it was hard to tell the extent of the damage he'd caused beneath all those white dressings. Today, I wasn't going to hide my appearance. I needed him to feel my pain and to know what he had done. I dressed in jeans and a tank top with a thin black sweater over it.

Mom arrived early to pick up Kess and me. Her voice was high-pitched, and she was talking fast. Her anxiety was palpable.

"Mom, it's going to be okay," I said. "This is going to be the end of it. We're not going to have to deal with this anymore."

"I know, I know," she said, rushing to the door when the bell rang. "It's going to be okay. It's going to be okay."

Mark Davis—the reporter from the *Valley News*—was at the door to ride with us to court. Jen was already there, taking photographs. When we were all ready, Kess led me through the garage and down the driveway. "Careful," she said. "The ground is slippery."

I put a little more pressure on the crook of Kess's arm. Twenty paces later, a car door opened, and I reached out to feel the cold, slick metal of the door. "I got it," I said, bending my knees and slipping inside. I had come a long way since leaving the hospital.

"Okay," Mom said, her voice fluttery. "Here we go. How are you feeling, Carm?"

"Now you're asking my questions for me," Mark teased, lightening the mood in the car.

"I feel like this is going to help me move forward," I said. "I can close this chapter and never look at it again. Oh—" I added. "Kess. Call Liza and tell her it's time to leave school."

There was a muffled rustling as Kess rifled through her bag. "Liza," she said. "Oh—you just saw us?" Kess laughed. "They're on the top of the hill," she said to us. "Okay. Just follow us to court, then."

We parked outside the court and regrouped with Liza and Hannah.

"Is anyone else here yet?" Hannah asked. My dad, brother, and sister-in-law were all meeting us there.

"I guess we'll see when we go inside," Kess said. "Carm, where do you want to sit?"

"The front row again," I said. "Girls, I want you to sit beside me. Can you do that?"

"Yeah, Mom," Liza said.

Hannah agreed, her voice stoic. "We'll be there."

I felt a surge of pride for my girls. They didn't sound remotely afraid, even though this was the first time they'd see Herb since the attack.

We all trooped inside, a small, awkwardly paced army. The heat was on inside the court; it wouldn't be long before I needed to remove my sweater. Past the entrance, a court employee led us to a room where we would be called when our case was up. We gathered together, trying to chat casually.

Then the prosecutor came into the room. He touched my shoulder reassuringly. "How are you feeling, Carmen?"

"I'm feeling good," I said.

"Good. Well, everyone else is getting here. Officer O'Donnell just arrived as well."

"Officer O'Donnell?" I gasped.

State Police Trooper Hugh O'Donnell had been the first responder. He wasn't on duty but lived just a quarter mile down the road. When he heard the call on his police scanner, he got dressed and rushed as fast as he could to my house. I didn't know what would have happened if he hadn't arrived when he did. He was a hero to me.

"Can I see him?" I asked. "I just want to say thank you."

"I can ask him to come in, but it has to be quick," the prosecutor said. "The hearing's about to start."

I waited impatiently, flustered with nerves and eagerness.

"Carm, he's coming," my mother said in a low voice.

Without sight, it was difficult to know whether to step forward or even what direction to turn my gaze. I stayed rooted in place, until I heard a male voice say, "Hello, Carmen."

"Officer O'Donnell," I said. A swift wave of emotion took the breath from my chest. All I could do was stretch my arms out until I touched him. Then I leaned forward, wrapping my arms around him. He was wearing a uniform and bulletproof vest; it was like embracing a rock. I cried a little when his arms circled me in return. "I just want you to know I appreciate what you did," I said. "You didn't have to come up. If you hadn't, I probably would have died. Thank you for saving my life."

We stood that way for a couple of seconds. As much as I wanted to look him in the eye while I expressed my gratitude, there was something freeing about only being able to *feel* these moments, without consideration of what this looked like to me, to others.

Quietly, simply, he said, "Thank you."

I smiled, as much as I could, as we pulled away. Before long, the prosecutor was letting us know it was time to go to the courtroom. "Mom," I whispered as we walked, "what did he look like?"

My mother's voice cracked. "His eyes were teary. He looked so in pain to see you this hurt."

My throat closed again as I followed Kess's lead into the courtroom. Soon, I was seated between her and the girls in the front row. There was a hushed murmur as family greeted family. Then I turned toward the front of the courtroom, shifting to get comfortable on the hard bench.

I leaned slightly toward Liza. "Let me know when he walks by."

Unlike the suppression hearing, my need to know when Herb was near wasn't urgent. I had already heard the heavy clanking of his chains, already pushed through the surreal fact of being in the same room without actually *seeing* him. Now it was more a matter of interest, like knowing where on my plate the green beans were located.

The room was silent when Liza nudged me. Sure enough, there was the eerie lumber of his footsteps. I turned in what I thought was his direction. Let him look at me. Let him see what he'd done. The footsteps quieted as he found his seat.

As the hearing began, the judge introduced herself, reviewed the case, and called several witnesses—including Officer O'Donnell—to the stand. The only detail that was omitted was my sexual assault. The prosecutor had thought it was in my best interest to leave that out and focus on the maiming. At the time, I was grateful. I didn't want my girls hearing those details, though I knew that

160

Liza had read every newspaper article about the attack.

"Will Carmen Blandin Tarleton take the stand?"

I came to attention. Kess slid out of the row first, and I followed, reaching for her arm. She guided me to the stand. As I took a seat, all I could think was, *Do I really have to say anything?* The evidence of what Herb had done was written all over my body. Kess slipped a tissue into my hands as she retreated back to the first row.

"Carmen, can you describe your pain to the court?" the prosecutor asked.

"I have pain every day," I said, wiping my mouth with the tissue. "Physical pain. And emotional as well, it goes without saying."

"Now, you've had a synthetic cornea transplant on your left eye," he said. "Is that correct?"

"Yes."

"And how much can you see now?"

"Almost nothing. I'm still legally blind."

"I'm going to stand in front of you," he said. After a pause, he asked, "Can you see me?"

"No."

I heard a soft footstep on the floor. "Can you see me now?"

"No."

Another footstep. I could sense that he was very close, but I could see nothing. "And how about now?" he asked.

"No."

"All right. What *can* you see?"

I looked down at the stand. Blurrily, I could make out a cylindrical shape. "I think there's a glass of water in front of me."

"Yes, there is."

"That's all I can see."

A few minutes of similar questions later, he was finished. "Thank you, Carmen," he said. His footsteps receded.

"No questions," I heard from the other side of the room. It was Kevin Griffin, Herb's attorney. I cringed, hearing his voice. He was a local man Herb had gone to when he tried to stop our divorce proceedings. Griffin hadn't had the time then to work with Herb, but after I got hurt, he was next in line to serve as state-appointed defense attorney. There was something unsettling to me about the fact that he'd met Herb before any of this had happened. I wasn't surprised he didn't cross-examine me. What could he possibly say?

"Ms. Blandin," the judge said to Kess, "you can help your sister off the stand now."

I waited for Kess's familiar hand and then followed her back to our seats. I'd only been on the stand for five or ten minutes. The tissue was ripped and moist in my hands.

There were more interviews after that, and the first hour stretched to two and then three. Fatigue was settling in. At some point, the judge read some of Herb's history. When I heard that he'd never graduated high school, I was accosted by a sense of startled anger. That was one more thing he had lied about.

"Does the defendant have anything he'd like to say to the court?" the judge asked, near the end.

I sat stock-still. While Herb had spoken briefly at the suppression hearing, I felt as though the last time I'd heard him talk was that night—so cool and *normal* as he asked if the thirty thousand dollars was worth all this. Would he speak now? Would he speak to *me*?

He cleared his throat. "I just want to say to the

162

girls—when I kicked in the door and if I hit one of you, I'm sorry. That was not my intention. I would never—" He sniffed hard, swallowed. "I would never hurt none of you."

His voice was different—shaky. It was as though he was struggling to push sound from his chest. My mind swirled. I couldn't believe this was the man I had been with—and loved—for nine years. I couldn't believe he had attacked me or that I was blind and disfigured. For a few moments, I existed in a surreal world, one parallel with but not touching the one I used to know.

"Carmen," he said.

My heart stopped.

"You didn't deserve it."

A few minutes later, before the judge gave her final sentencing, she said to Herb, "To say you didn't mean to hurt one of those girls doesn't make sense. You were hurting their mother, which was hurting them."

Herb had no reply.

"I remand you to the commission of corrections for a period of not less than thirty years and not more than seventy years for the crime of maiming," she said. "You are ineligible for parole for a minimum of thirty years."

Without realizing I'd been holding my breath, I released it in a long sigh of relief. The courtroom was dead silent. No one clapped or shouted words of victory or lament. (Who would lament? Not surprisingly, Herb's family was nowhere to be found. If they knew about what he had done, I had no idea.) There was no rejoicing until after court was adjourned and my family and I were escorted into a back room. Then the energy erupted. The girls laughed and joked with my father and brother, and the air seemed light and fizzy. It was like my daughters had been able to release the negativity—the negativity we adults so cling to—as easily as shrugging off a sweater, and it made me appreciate them even more.

"It's over, Mom!" Liza hugged me, and I held her back. The feeling of joy was so intense that I was almost glad to be blind, experiencing it in all its undiluted force.

"You know, you guys don't have to go back to school if you don't want to," I said.

"No, Mom," Liza said. "I want to go back."

"Hannah? What about you?"

"I want to go back, too."

"Well, all right then," I said. "You'd better get out of here."

They hugged me again before they left, and I wondered if they recognized what they were doing: naturally, seemingly without conscious thought, they were taking their own power back. They weren't letting Herb's sentencing change the way they lived their daily lives. I was proud of them.

Voices rose excitedly, and I knew that the prosecutor had entered the room. I felt as though I was beaming, though I wasn't sure what my smile looked like anymore. "Well done, Carmen," he said. "I hope everything goes well for you. If there's anything I can do for you, let me know."

I gave him a quick, impulsive hug. "Thank you. For everything."

The room pulsed with energy for a few minutes longer until we all dispersed and headed to our cars.

"So," Mark asked on our way home, "how are you feeling now, Carmen?"

I let myself relax in my seat. "I feel lighter," I said. "I feel like I can put this aside now."

Later that night, we all watched the news segment on

the sentencing. There came Herb's voice again from the speakers: "… and if I hit one of you, I'm sorry. That was not my intention."

"How did you guys feel about that?" I asked. "That he apologized to you, I mean."

Hannah was quiet, but Liza spoke up. "It did make me feel better that he said he was sorry," she ventured.

I didn't say anything. I wasn't going to take that away from them. If they took it as a sincere apology, and it helped them, I was glad. With hindsight, Herb probably did the best he could that day. At the time, though, I was disappointed. Some part of me needed to know that he regretted what he did to me. He'd said I didn't deserve it, but he never said he was sorry.

Regardless, it was the sense of completion I'd been yearning for. Someday, a lot of what made life so difficult for me would fade, and one of those things already had: I no longer had to worry about Herb. He was going to pay his debt, whereas I was not going to stay imprisoned by what he did to me. I didn't feel that my gratification at his sentencing was vengeful. At the time, it felt like justice.

CHAPTER 15

I
ONCE
WAS
BLIND

IN APRIL 2009, KESS HAD BEEN LIVING WITH THE girls and me for over a year. Her devotion to my care will always humble me, but I was ready to live on my own with Liza and Hannah—and Kess was no doubt ready to move forward with her own life. She was forty-two and finishing her doctoral dissertation. Now she was work-ing part-time for the Association for Alzheimer's in New Hampshire. She had her dreams to fulfill.

When Kess left, the only open wounds still left on my body were on my head and behind my arms on my back. I occasionally broke the skin on my lower legs, but those dressings I could handle myself. For the others, Kess came up two or three times a week to help. Regaining even a small sense of independence felt wonderful. I hoped the next phase would come later that month, with my second synthetic cornea transplant. This time, Dr. Melki was going to replace my damaged right cornea. Since my right eye had been stronger all along, Dr. Melki was optimistic that the results would be better than the underwhelming first surgery.

The night before I left for Boston, Liza's nine-year-old cat, Sonny, wasn't acting right. He'd been sick for a while, lethargic and shaky, and now he refused to emerge from beneath Liza's bed. Liza was teary as she called for him. Then she asked, "Mom, do you think he's going to die?"

I hesitated. I did think he was going to die, and I knew I wouldn't be there for Liza when he did. I'd be in the hospital again. No mother wants her child to face mortality alone, and I felt swollen with frustration at my injuries and my never-ending hospital visits that made me less available to my daughters.

"Take him to the vet tomorrow, okay? They'll know more than me what's wrong with him."

"Okay," Liza sniffled. My heart broke, imagining her running her fingers through Sonny's dull coat as he shook on an examining table. *Please hang on,* I thought, *so I can be with her.*

The next day, I woke up at a quarter to six and went through my slow process of getting dressed. My mother and Kess arrived a few minutes later. Kess would be going with me to Boston while my mother stayed with the girls. Before we left, I hugged Liza and Hannah goodbye. I could sense Liza's sadness and wished I could give her a kiss, but my mouth didn't pucker.

"Good luck, Mom," Hannah said. "Maybe you'll be able to see us when you get back!"

"Maybe," I said, "but let's not get too excited."

My yearning for sight was so painful that I couldn't let myself access hope for this surgery's success. With my left eye, all I could see was hand movement—*if* it was directly in front of my eye. My vision had never improved after that first brilliant flash of magenta.

"Don't forget to take Sonny to the vet today," I told Liza, as if she needed reminding.

"I won't," she said. "Bye, Mom. We'll see you tomorrow."

Kess and I drove forty minutes until we reached the Dartmouth Coach station in Lebanon. Then, as we'd done countless times before, we boarded the bus for the three-hour ride to Boston.

While I was in surgery, Liza dropped Sonny off at the vet. She went to school that day and called the vet afterward to check up on him. Sure enough, Sonny was dying. On her own, Liza decided to put her cat to sleep. She asked that they cremate him and, that afternoon, took Sonny home in a little urn. When I returned the next day, my right eye covered, she said, "I hope you don't mind, but the bill was five hundred for the vet and two hundred to cremate him."

I hugged her. "I'm so sorry you had to deal with that by yourself," I said. "I know how hard that must have been. I'm proud of you. Of course I don't mind."

As difficult as it was, that was one of those times I had to trust that if I wasn't there for Liza, she didn't need me to be.

○ ○ ○

Ten days after surgery, I was brushing my teeth in the bathroom. My mouth was so tight that the stretch tugged the skin down on my right eye; that was when I caught a glimpse of silver: the faucet.

"No," I whispered. It couldn't be. I opened my mouth again, and again there was that beautiful silver tube extending from the sink. It was the faucet, gleaming. The colors were vivid, dazzling to my new cornea. How had I not noticed them before? I wanted to laugh and cry and shout to everyone that my sight was back, but I was still wary. This could be a momentary fluke. In fact, that was probably what it was. I convinced myself of that, because to believe my vision had returned meant I had something to lose again. I had lost so much already. So I said nothing. I just thought, *Please let me see my children one more time. If I go blind after that, so be it. Just let me see them again.*

Over the next few days, more drainage cleared from my eye, and I couldn't deny anymore that my sight was returning. The excitement was choking, overwhelming. For the first time since my first cornea transplant, I let myself hope. Maybe it would keep getting better. Maybe I'd be able to *drive* again one day. The idea of sitting behind the wheel of a car, my foot on the gas pedal, was thrilling.

I decided to surprise my family with my sight. While I waited for the girls to get home (what did my daughters look like?), I called my father. He was at work, so my call went to voicemail. "Dad, this is Carm," I said. "I'd like for you to stop by because I would really like to see you." I placed only slightly more emphasis than normal on the word *see*. "Okay, talk to you later!"

Time passed quickly as I rushed clumsily around the house, reacquainting myself with the large, still-blurry shapes of furniture and paintings on the walls. I was ecstatic. Then I heard the key turn in the door: Hannah was home.

"Hey, Mom!" she called. Her footsteps treaded into the kitchen.

My heart pounded as I made my way toward her after-school sounds. I saw her shape by the counter; already,

I was almost weeping with joy. "Hannah," I said, my voice breaking. She turned quickly, alarmed at first, and I said, "I can see you."

"What?" she exclaimed. "You can?"

"Come here," I said. "Come close."

She hurried over to me, and I neared within six inches of her face. When I saw her smile, I burst into tears. Her face had thinned in the last two years, and I marveled at her blue eyes and dark hair. Her profile was sweet and pretty, cheeks curved with her smile. "Oh, my God," I said. "You're beautiful! You look so much older!"

Hannah laughed, throwing her arms around me. "You can really see me, can't you?"

"Yes!"

I hugged her back, crying. I wanted to live in this moment forever.

"Have you told anyone else yet?" she asked.

"No, I'm going to surprise them."

Liza came home later that evening, and I wasted no time before closing the gap between my face and hers. "I can see you!" I said, my eyes filling with tears again. At sixteen, Liza had changed less than Hannah had, but I was still astounded at how much like a woman she looked. I touched her face and wavy hair, soaking her in.

"Oh, that's great!" Liza said, laughing. "That's so great, Mom!"

Kess was next up. She was stopping by the following day with some groceries, and when I spoke to her on the phone, I said nothing about my sight. When she nudged the door open, gripping two cloth bags, I walked right up to her and took one from her hand. I followed her to the kitchen.

"Are you seeing better today?" Kess asked cautiously.

"Well, let's see," I said. Nonchalantly, I lifted the grocery bag closer to my face and began reading the letters on the side: "P-L-E-A-S-E R-E-N-E-W—"

Kess shrieked. "You can see! Carm, you can see!" She grabbed me, and I fell against her, and we screamed and danced around the kitchen like kids. We were alone in the house, free to let our wild happiness emerge how it chose.

"Yes, yes, yes!" I screeched back. "Look how much I can see!"

I tried to catch my breath as I read what I could off the grocery bag. "'Renew, re-use, recycle!' I mean, they're big letters, but still—I can see!"

"Oh, Carm," she said, "this is so wonderful."

Kess gazed at me, and I gazed back. I hadn't seen her since November of 2006. She was thin, with shoulder-length dark hair and warm brown eyes gleaming with tears. *Girl, you're as pretty as you always were!* I thought. In those moments, I knew Kess was completely sharing in my joy. She always did, any time something good happened in my life. She celebrated my happiness as if it were her own.

My parents were less overtly joyful. I had told my mother on the phone that she needed to come over because I could see, and when she did, she was a bit numb. I hugged her tightly. "I haven't seen you in years, and I was afraid I never would again," I said.

"This is so great, Carm!" she said, but her enthusiasm seemed tempered with hesitation. I thought she must be scared for me, scared that I would lose this gift, and I understood her fear.

My dad called later, saying he'd gotten my message

and was going to stop by.

"Dad, did you *get* my message, though?" I asked. "I said I'd *see* you later, because I can see you now!"

Dad was in his late sixties, a handsome man with Native-American features. "Oh, Dad, you're still a hottie," I teased when I saw him. Dad's reaction echoed Mom's, and though a part of me wished everyone could react like Kess and the girls, I recognized that they were probably overwhelmed. All people react differently to life-changing news. I wasn't going to dwell on the fact that they didn't jump around and scream with me.

The final person I planned to surprise was Dr. Melki. It was less than two weeks after the surgery, and I was returning for a follow-up visit. By then, I was no longer worried about losing my sight. It was so real, so vivid, that my fear of loss had disappeared with my blindness.

"Mom," I said, "lead me around like I can't see."

"Carm, you're so bad," Mom said, but there was a smile in her voice.

We walked into Boston Laser, Dr. Melki's clinic, with the gait we'd become so practiced at—me holding onto Mom's elbow, echoing the rhythm of her steps. Dr. Melki was inside, and I tried not to look at him when he said, "Carmen, how are you doing?"

"Good," I said.

"Good. See you in a minute."

He gave a little wave as he retreated from the waiting room. Mom and I were called back a few minutes later, and I took her arm again as we followed a nurse into an exam room. When the door opened and Dr. Melki came in, I walked toward him and touched his arm. "You know," I said, "it is so good to finally see you."

There was a moment of silence, and then Dr. Melki's face broke into a cheek-splitting smile. His eyes filled with tears as he leaned in to hug me tightly. Mom watched us, smiling and wiping her eyes. I felt like a part of a team that had just won a championship.

"Come on, Carmen." Dr. Melki offered me his arm as if he were asking me to dance. "Let me walk you to another examining room." We walked arm in arm down the hall, though we both knew I no longer needed the guidance. It was the tenderest moment I'd ever shared with him.

"Let me ask you to read the chart, Carmen," Dr. Melki said in the next room.

Excitedly, I read out the top two lines.

"That is excellent. Your vision is 20/200—right at the border of legally blind. I'm confident I can bring you down to 20/100, which would classify you as visually impaired."

"Oh, that is so good!" I said. "I can't wait."

As the joy settled, there was one more thing I needed to do: look at myself. My vision wasn't clear enough to see myself in the mirror at a glance; I would need to do a more intentional self-examination. At the time, I had no idea what I looked like. I could tell from the pain of my dressing changes that my wounds were still severe, and I always made sure the girls never saw me changing or showering; I thought seeing my naked body would be horrifying for them. Hell, I thought it'd be horrifying for me. The depth of my self-consciousness, once I was on the verge of validating it, was staggering.

Finally, I gathered the courage to close my bathroom door and pick up a hand mirror. I sat on the closed lid of the toilet, breathing deeply to calm myself. My hand trembled as I lifted the mirror to my face. In my mind, I could hear that deep TV voice resonating: "Warning: the images you are about to see are graphic ..."

At first, my brain didn't register what I was seeing. Then the pieces came crashing together: a very white face, mottled with scars. Misshapen nose. Missing ear. Lips and eyes that bore no resemblance to my own. "Oh, God," I whispered. I had known, intellectually, that I was disfigured—but what I hadn't realized was that there was no Carmen left in my face. Carmen was gone.

Thirty seconds was all I could bear. I dropped my hand back into my lap, overwhelmed with a crushing sense of loss. Where was I, if not in the mirror? How was I supposed to think of myself? How had my family adapted to seeing me this way? In the solitude of my bathroom, I let myself cry.

For the next few days, I looked at myself as much as I could stand: thirty seconds, lower the mirror, breathe. Forty-five seconds, lower the mirror, breathe. I mourned the loss of my physical self but, as with all mourning, I felt it would get better over time—if I faced it. I asked Kess to take a picture of me, and Liza printed it out on regular eight-by-ten computer paper.

"What do you want this for?" she asked curiously. She and Hannah were sitting at the kitchen table.

"I want to get a better look at myself."

"Mom ..."

I had been given a magnifying machine that I could use to read my bills and other documents, and I laid the photo of myself beneath the lens. I didn't think it would bother me any more than seeing my face in the mirror. I was wrong. All I could see, when I looked down, was a stranger. A severely disfigured stranger. Just like that, I knew why the little girl had cried on the bus. I knew why Mom and Kess had been unable to describe me. I was utterly unrecognizable.

"Mom?" Liza asked. "Are you okay?"

"No," I said. "My god, this sucks. It really sucks."

I turned away from the magnifying machine and walked to my room, my new vision cloudy with tears. I closed my bedroom door and sat at the edge of my bed. Even as I wept, I regretted letting my kids see that reaction. But there was nothing else I could do.

○ ○ ○

Because my experiences with the *Valley News* were so positive, I had agreed weeks before to do a story with a major publication about my cornea transplant. As soon as the reporter walked into my house and I shook her hand, I got a strange feeling. By the time we sat down for the interview, I recognized it as wariness. Though I still couldn't make out faces, the reporter was standoffish, a bit cold. There were times she spoke to the photographer instead of me: "See if you can get a shot of her from that angle."

Later, she asked, "So, tell me ... what happened that night?"

"I'm sorry," I said. "I don't want to discuss that. I thought we were here to talk about the cornea transplant."

"Right. Well, do you have any photos of you from before?"

I was prepared with a bucket of photographs. "Just don't use the picture on top with my brother in it. He doesn't like being in the news."

She ignored me. "Oh, this is a good one," she said to

the photographer.

"Did you hear what I said? Don't use that one with my brother."

"We can crop him out," she assured me.

I said that was okay, and they left soon after. The feeling of unease remained.

Sure enough, when the article was published, my brother wasn't cropped out. The reporter had also taken "creative liberties" with my story. She wrote about the "dark man" I had seen standing in the back of Liza's room, which was incorrect, and I seethed at what felt like a violation of my personal story. How dare she just *make things up*? The worst part, though, was that she went behind my back to try to talk to Herb. Of course, the prison system didn't allow her in, and a victims' advocate called me right after she left. I immediately called the reporter.

"You don't do something like that without telling me!" I exploded. "You don't go try to get 'his side' of things— this was supposed to be a story about my eyesight, about Dr. Melki and my cornea transplant. This isn't some investigative journalism piece. What were you thinking?"

She apologized, but it didn't ease my indignation. I called her editor to complain. When he didn't answer, I left a message asking that he call me back to discuss the story I'd just done with that particular reporter. He returned my call several days later, but I knew instantly that he wasn't going to side with me.

"I'm sorry her actions upset you," he said pleasantly. "She was just trying to be thorough."

"Thorough," I scoffed. "That wasn't being thorough. Please don't call me for other stories. I'm not interested in working with your paper again."

My mother shook her head when I told her what had happened. "This is why ordinary people shouldn't mess with the media," she said.

"They just screw you over," others agreed.

There were times I wondered if they were right. Could I do this? Was it too hard to take care of myself because I couldn't see people? But I believed so strongly that everything had happened for a reason, and if I stayed aware of what that path might be, everything would work out. I was just learning the business of the media, I reminded myself. *And* I was learning how to trust my intuition in an entirely different way. Mistakes were bound to happen.

As a nurse, I knew how to gauge and trust my intuition, and it had always served me well. But in personal relationships, my weakness had always been becoming blinded by my affection for someone. When I fell in love, I was smitten. In other relationships, I was naïve. While my brother was able to say, after one interaction with the reporter, "Are you sure you want to work with her? She doesn't seem sincere," I argued that she was young and perhaps inexperienced. The truth was, though, that I had felt the same misgiving from the beginning. I needed to trust the little voice trying to guide me. That was my big lesson: I had more power than I was accessing. I could pick and choose whom I worked with. *I* was in control. That felt like growth to me.

○ ○ ○

Three weeks later, I returned to Dr. Melki for another follow-up. This time, my vision was 20/400. I had lost some of the detail I could see before.

"It's probably okay," Dr. Melki said, "but I want to see you in another three weeks to make sure."

For the next ten days, the sky hung gray and low. The weather worked in my favor, since direct light was painful to my undilating pupils. Still, in preparation for the summer, I had asked my friend Kathie to order me new curtains. She chose some beautiful, thick drapes, and she and Bill came over to hang them one afternoon. Kathie directed Bill as he began hooking the heavy material over the rod, and I sat and watched their blurry shapes move.

"No," Kathie snapped. "Not like that. The hooks go the other way. The curtains will fall if she pulls them to the side too hard."

Bill grunted. "They look right to me."

"No, look at the picture. Clearly, they—" Kathie stopped herself and looked in my direction. She gave a self-conscious laugh. "Jesus, look at me. Here I am, giving Bill a hard time about nothing. It seems so silly after what you've been through."

I felt a flash of irritation. "Kathie, it's fine. Just be normal." It had been two years since the attack, and I was so tired of things not being *normal*. With Kathie, I wanted my longtime girlfriend back, not someone who was afraid to speak around me.

"No, really. I'm sorry. I need to think before I open my mouth sometimes."

I sighed.

On July 8, I returned to see Dr. Melki. "How's your vision been lately, Carmen?" he asked.

"A bit dark, to be honest. I still can't see detail as well. It could be the weather, though," I offered. "I also just got some new curtains that block out the light."

"Hmm," Dr. Melki said. He used a small penlight to peer into my eye and then asked me to look into several different machines. The longer the exam took, the more knotted my stomach became.

"Is something wrong?" I asked.

"I hate to say it, but yes," he said. "You're having a complication from the surgery."

"What is it?"

"Sometimes, scar tissue can grow behind the cornea and needs to be excised with a laser. I want you to go to Mass Eye and Ear immediately and see a retina specialist. Her name is Dr. Lucy Young. I'll call ahead and make sure they're ready for you."

"Am I going to lose my sight?"

"Let's see." Dr. Melki never said yes until it was done.

Two days later, I made the exhausting day trip back to Boston to see Dr. Young. She ran some tests on my eye and then did an ultrasound to get a better look. Afterward, she sat across from me with a sense of heaviness that told me everything I needed to know.

"I have some hard news," she said. "The scar tissue is infiltrating your retina. You're going to lose your vision if we don't try surgery."

My throat closed. "Lose it completely?"

"There's no regaining what you've lost, but there's a sixty percent chance I can save what sight you still have with surgery."

I could still see faces if I got close enough, though not in as much detail as before. I would do anything to keep my vision from worsening. "Okay. What does it involve?"

Dr. Young explained that they would cut out the scar tissue and put a gas bubble in my eye to hold the retina in place. I would need to remain in a face-down position for four weeks in order for the bubble to actually press against my retina.

"I can do that," I said. "How soon can we schedule it?"

∘ ∘ ∘

The next day, Kathie called and I told her what Dr. Young had said. "I just don't understand why this is happening," I said, hating how small and sad my voice sounded.

"Have you been taking your afternoon medications?" Kathie asked.

"What? Didn't you hear what I said? I'm going blind. I'm losing my vision."

"Yes, I know," Kathie said. "And I'm very sorry about that, but I just can't deal with it."

"Okay, Kathie," I said, defeated. "I'll call you some other time."

Ten days later, I returned to Mass Ear and Eye Infirmary—swiftly becoming my second home—for surgery. The vision in my right eye had deteriorated tremendously. I was desperate for the procedure to work.

After surgery, I felt as though I was on a boat, the room dipping and lifting around me. I retched as the anesthesia wore off, and someone gave me medicine to ease me into sleep. When I awoke again, my right eye was covered. It was nine or ten o'clock at night, and Kess was in the room. Right away, I knew something was wrong.

"Kess," I said, "I'm not face-down. Dr. Young said when I woke up I would be face-down."

"Carm," Kess said. "Maybe we should wait for the doctors to come back."

"Tell me. What happened?"

The room was silent. "She couldn't put the gas bubble in your eye."

"Why not?"

"There was so much scar tissue that it wasn't even worth it. She said it was three hundred and sixty degrees—it engulfed your whole eye."

Oh, God. "So … I am going to go blind."

I heard movement, and then one side of the bed dipped with Kess's weight. I scooted over slightly, and she crawled into bed beside me. I turned my body toward her warmth. Holding each other, all we could do was cry.

The next day, I awoke with the jarring, heavy sense of despair one feels after a death. This was more than unfair. How much more suffering could I take?

"Carm." Kess slipped a phone into my hand in the hospital bed. "You need to call Mom and tell her you're okay. She's not going to California anymore because she's so upset."

My mother had been planning a trip to LA to visit my younger sister, Rachel. When she answered, her voice sounded as anguished as I felt. "Mom, you need to go see Rachel and have a good time," I said. "I'm fine. I promise."

"Carm, you're not fine. You've lost your sight."

"I know that," I said, more harshly than I had intended. "Look, I'm going to stay with Kess this week. I'm okay. Go to California."

"Are you sure? Honey, I can stay with you."

"No, Mom. I'm sure."

The truth was, I didn't want to deal with anyone else's pain or pity over my blindness. I wanted to deal with this in my own way. I needed to reach a place of understanding about why this had happened. A part of me felt as though

I had no grounds for complaint; after all, I'd said that if I could just see my children one more time, I could accept going blind again. But, as with most of us, a taste of what my future could look like hadn't been enough. I thought back to just a few weeks ago. The hope that I could drive again and achieve some kind of independence was still fresh in my mind. It seemed impossible that it had been taken away so quickly.

I saw my therapist several times throughout the next few months, but ultimately, I just wanted to be alone.

As my world quite literally darkened, I slipped into a depression, where every feeling of sadness or grief was amplified. The senses I did have only reminded me of what I missed. Every time I heard my kids laugh, I ached to see their smiles. When the sun warmed my skin, I thought of the garden I used to tend all spring, my hands plunged deep in the dark, moist soil. A car horn reminded me that I would never again drive to the grocery store, let alone drop my girls off at college one day. The litany of lost things was endless. It was a hole I could have tumbled through, limb over limb, forever.

Ten days after the unsuccessful surgery, I went back to see Dr. Melki. I was heavy hearted as my mother and I walked back inside his clinic; this time, I held her arm out of necessity.

When Dr. Melki walked into the exam room, we both said a quiet hello.

"How are *you* doing?" I asked. I knew he was going to take the failed transplant personally, and I wanted him to know that I didn't blame him.

"I'm all right, Carmen. I'm all right. And you?"

"I'm okay," I said, but I was crying.

Dr. Melki leaned in to hug me. "We all have a lot to learn from your strength," he said in a low voice.

By September, only four months after I first saw the silver gleam of my bathroom faucet, I was completely blind in my right eye. All I could see was light if it was exceptionally bright and movement if it was directly in front of my eye. Otherwise, it was pure, inky, endless blackness. That was when I started talking to Dr. Melki about using contact lenses to cover the transplant on my left eye. When I lost my corneas, I lost the protective lenses that covered them. So, when the synthetic cornea had been placed in my left eye the previous July, I was given a lens—similar to a typical contact—that would keep it from being exposed to air. However, the lens was big and bulky and held drainage that kept me from seeing as well as I thought I could. Dr. Melki agreed to let me use regular contact lenses, which gave me a little improvement but not enough to counteract my overall disappointment.

About that time, Jen and Mark from the *Valley News* wanted to continue with me for another few months to see what my sight would become. I couldn't do it.

"You need to end it," I told them when they came up to see me shortly before the girls' school year began.

"Well," Jen hedged, "we're not really in a place where we can do that. We haven't reached the conclusion we were hoping for."

My voice broke. "It's been almost a year, Jen. I know me going blind isn't where you want to end it, but I've got too many things to deal with right now. It's too heavy for me."

Jen sighed. "I wish you would reconsider."

"I can't. I appreciate what you're doing for me, helping

to tell my story, but I need to be alone right now." I was sorry to disappoint them, but this felt like acting out the lesson I'd learned with the other reporter: I was setting boundaries, doing what was best for *me*.

In November of 2009, the *Valley News* published a five-part series about me. Each piece was a combination of Jen's photos and Mark's words, and they did a beautiful job of describing what I had been through in the previous year—what I had survived. I had no regrets about letting them into my life; they treated my story with respect, and even in my grief, the series gave me hope that it would inspire others to work through tragedy.

With everything going on surrounding my vision, I had set aside my Disfigurement Challenge. Then came a day late that year. With nothing specific prompting it, I found myself crying. More than anything, I wanted to accept the way I looked. It wasn't going to change, and feeling bad about it was standing in the way of other things I wanted to do. Despite ending the *Valley News* series, I still wanted to share my story. I was thinking about public speaking one day and about writing a book. I knew I wasn't physically or emotionally ready for any of that, but I also didn't want disfigurement weighing on my mind anymore. It didn't feel good. So, that day, it came to a head.

In mid-afternoon, the front door opened and Kess called out, "Carm, it's me!"

I didn't respond. I was lost in the heaviness of my emotions. Kess found me on the couch, where I'd been weeping for hours.

"Carm, what is it?" She rushed to me, took my hands. "What's happened?"

"It just really sucks to look like this," I choked.

"Oh, Carm." Kess wrapped her arms around me, and I cried into her shoulder. Before long, I could feel her body shaking. Once again I realized how Herb hadn't just hurt me; he'd hurt all of us.

"I want to get over it so badly," I said. "I just don't know how."

I cried like a baby in Kess's arms and then for the remainder of that afternoon and evening. Though I was no stranger to tears, I hadn't cried for this continuous a period in months—maybe ever. It wasn't until later that I realized how much negativity I was releasing through my lament. In some way, I was freeing up space in my body and mind for new ways of thinking.

It was shocking and I didn't know how I had done it, but shortly after that day I no longer cared how I looked. I had somehow broken through my Disfigurement Challenge. It was *so* liberating! The most amazing part was that once I stopped feeling bad about my appearance, people responded to me differently. When I was out in public and little kids were around, they didn't cry. They *hugged* me.

"Kess," I said in awe, "I'm not scaring people anymore."

Kess laughed. "No, you're sure not."

It struck me that people reacted to the way I felt about myself. When I felt like a monster, I was perceived as a monster. When I felt good, I was a woman again; I was just scarred. It showed me we are all entirely in control of the way others see us. Energy is everything.

The lesson was powerful. I finally realized that I had to make a choice: I could keep sinking into grief over my blindness, or I could appreciate the sight I did have in my left eye. It wasn't much, but even distinguishing the wave of a hand—the color of a tank top—was *something*. What if I lost that? It would join the list of things I wished I had appreciated at the time. And when I had regained my eyesight and thought, *Just let me see my kids again*, I limited myself. I would never make that mistake again. When something good happened, I would take it *all*. I would enjoy it and love it, not fearing the possibility of loss. I intuitively sensed the freedom of living that way.

Choosing to feel grateful for what sight remained saved me from my darkness. In December, I went back to visit Dr. Melki. The contact lens I'd been using had been falling out for months. There were days Kess had to come over and help me slip it in, and others when I realized the lens had been out of my eye for several days. By the time I saw Dr. Melki, I knew something was wrong.

"Carmen, it looks like it has been exposed to air," Dr. Melki said. "I need to replace the whole transplant."

It was strange, but I could tell in his body language that he was *happy*. He was holding my chart against his chest, bouncing on the balls of his feet. Dr. Melki was not a bouncer.

"What do you think about that?" I asked.

"I think I can do a better job. I'm going to schedule another doctor to come in and see you. Just give me one minute." He set my chart down on the counter as he left the room.

I turned toward Kess. "What does the chart say?"

"Carm!" Kess said, laughing. But she went over to the counter and read it out loud. "'Corneal melt.'"

"What does that mean? Why do you think he's so happy?"

"Like he said," Kess answered, "he thinks he can do a better job."

o o o

Sure enough, when I woke up in the recovery room later that month, Dr. Melki said the words every post-op patient wants to hear: "Everything went smoothly."

"Will I be able to see?" I asked groggily.

"Not for a while," he said. "Your eye bled during the operation, and it's going to take a while for all that blood to reabsorb. We'll know more about how much sight you can expect after that."

I'm going to miss Christmas again, I thought, before falling back to sleep.

For the next month, all I could see was floating blood; it looked like an abstract painting, as though someone had flicked scarlet paint from a brush onto the canvas in no discernable pattern. As a nurse, looking at the world through a veil of blood didn't bother me; it was the question of what my vision would be that was haunting: would it be better than the 20/600 it was before? Worse? I hoped it wouldn't be worse. Already, I was struggling to pay my own bills. Every few days, I went to my magnifying machine and placed my checkbook under the glass, straining to see the lines. I couldn't.

Appreciate, I reminded myself. While I knew a surgical complication had robbed me of sight in my right eye, I also felt it was to teach me a lesson of patience and appreciation. I couldn't worry about blindness any longer. I would just wait for the blood to clear. I would use whatever sight was left the best I could and be grateful to have anything at all.

During my period of waiting, I had a visit from my friend George from the Phoenix Society of Burn Survivors. It was two days after Christmas, and snow whitened the trees and ground outside. George sold insurance, and he always gave me a call when he was visiting clients in Vermont.

The house was toasty warm when he came over, with the Christmas tree still up and a feeling of lazy relaxation in the air. My mother came over every day since Kess had moved out and I couldn't see anything but blood. I tried to be optimistic, telling George about the surgery and what I hoped from my eyesight.

"I'm just working on being patient," I said.

"Patience is the key," he agreed.

Later, the subject changed to the World Burn Conference, an annual event that drew hundreds of burn survivors and their families. George was talking about some of the conference sessions and attendees—about how they had found happiness through their recovery.

"There's always that forgiveness factor," he said. "For people like you, I mean, who have been hurt by the hands of someone else."

His voice was soft and kind, and I was startled by his words. Forgiveness? Aside from my mother and Kess telling me they'd had to forgive Herb early on, no one had mentioned the word in relation to *me* forgiving. I hadn't even thought about it. After George left, though, it was like a tickle in the back of my throat. I tried to swallow past it, but it was impossible to ignore.

CHAPTER 16

NIGHT
IS
DARKEST

IN THE FIRST WEEK OF 2010, I WOKE UP . . . AND THE blood was gone. I couldn't see detail, but I could see color and shapes and outlines! I could see light and dark and, way up close, the spirited sparkle in both my girls' eyes. Though my vision wasn't as clear as my right eye had been, it was better than it was before the surgery. That was all I wanted, and this time, I was placing no restrictions on my joy. Through all my loss, I was starting to feel blessed. Patience was not about idle waiting; it was about pausing long enough to seek understanding. If my right eye had kept its vision, perhaps I never would have learned to appreciate what I had when I had it. It was a powerful lesson.

As I settled into life with just the sight I needed to get by, I turned my attention to my finances. I was drowning. The money from the sale of our California house was long gone, and social security covered only the bare minimum of my family's needs. What would I do if I stopped being able to pay my two mortgages? I had Liza and Hannah to consider, and what about saving for their college funds? At this point, the concept of any savings at all was almost laughable.

Finally, I got a call from my insurance company: they were offering me a settlement for my long-term disability that was close to fifty thousand dollars. We couldn't live on that forever, but at the time it seemed like the answer to a prayer. Overjoyed, I took the settlement and breathed a huge sigh of relief. We would be okay for a while longer.

With sight in my left eye continuing to improve—I was 20/400!—I was finally able to do something that had been long out of reach: read. One of the first pieces of paper (besides bills) I slid under my magnifying machine was a letter. It was from a man named Alan. My first love.

I had just turned fifteen when Alan and I started seeing each other. He was significantly older than I was, and I snuck out of the house on weekends so my mother wouldn't find out. We drove up the dirt roads on the Appalachian Trail in Pomfret, Vermont, sitting on the hood of his car until two in the morning. The sky was an unbroken black bowl above us as we kissed and talked. He was a reader, so he lent me book after book, and we sat shoulder-to-shoulder dissecting them.

"I really liked this one," I offered, holding Ruth Montgomery's *Strangers Among Us.* The cover was bright red and purple with swirling clouds. There was something mysterious about it.

"What did you like about it?" Alan took the book from my hands and opened it to a random page. He scanned it quickly, with familiarity.

"Just this idea about 'walk-ins,'" I said. "Enlightened beings entering the minds of people who will be leaving the earth soon. She says Gandhi is one. Isn't that crazy?"

"Do you believe that?"

I shrugged. I was neither religious nor particularly spiritual, but I liked the idea of such "beings" borrowing normal people's bodies, leading the rest of us to some enlightened future. "If I knew I was going to die soon," I said, "I would give one of them permission to use me to help others. Why not?"

Alan and I were together for a year before small-town rumors reached my mother's ears.

"You're not going to believe what I heard at work today," she said, laughingly incredulous.

I glanced up at her from the couch. "What?"

"That you're seeing Alan." She shook her head, setting her purse down on a table by the door. "Can you imagine that?"

"Actually," I said, with a sixteen-year-old's casual defiance, "I can. Because it's true."

My mother gaped at me. "Oh, Carmen. Tell me you're kidding. He's a grown man! You're still a child."

"Mom, I'm not a child, and I know what I'm doing." I rose from the couch and slipped my feet into old sneakers. "He's good to me, he really is. We're in love."

Eventually, Alan moved a couple hours north to Burlington. I drove my car up to see him each weekend, loving the independence that came with those trips. Our relationship stayed strong for a few years—but he was, after all, a man. I thought he was possibly seeing other women his own age. Sure enough, when I was a senior, Alan broke up with me. The heartbreak was sharp and sudden, like a crystal glass fallen to the floor. I had so little comprehension as to what had happened. Had he simply gotten tired of me? Was I that disposable?

To get over Alan, I started dating another guy a few

months later. It was no help; my heart was not open to someone new. It turned out, at least in the short term, that Alan's wasn't either. One rainy November weekend, he was in White River visiting a friend and invited me over to talk. I ran a brush through my hair and pulled on some clean jeans, my tomboy version of dressing up. For the fifteen-minute drive, I ran through scenarios in my mind. What would I say if he asked me back? That had to be what he wanted to talk about, right? I imagined him pulling me close, telling me what a mistake he had made by breaking up with me. "I miss you," he'd say. "I was stupid. Please forgive me."

My teenaged daydreams weren't far off.

In his friend Ray's dining area, the three of us sat at the table while Alan and Ray got stoned. I didn't smoke with them. I thought I might fall in love all over again if I did, with nothing stopping me from gazing into Alan's light blue eyes or running my fingers through his curly, rusty brown hair. I kept my emotional distance as we all talked. Half an hour later, Ray excused himself to go to the store.

"Carmen," Alan said. His eyes were already welling with tears.

"No," I said.

"Take me back," he said. "I love you."

I was still so hurt and angry. I wanted him to know that he couldn't just have me when he wanted me and cast me aside when he didn't. "No," I said. "You made your choice. Now you're just going to have to live with it."

Even as I stalked out of Ray's house, I regretted it. My chest seared as I fumbled with my car keys, and what young intuition I had told me to go back. I was seventeen, though, and prideful. I twisted the key to unlock the door, slid into my seat, and drove away without looking back.

The next fall, I happened to be passing Ray's house on my way out of White River. From a distance, I saw Alan's red Toyota Celica in the driveway, half-covered by some shrubbery. In a second, all of my old feelings rushed back. I remembered our nights of long talks and making love, how I reveled in the experience of learning about the world. On impulse, I parked at the curb. A quick mirror check ensured that I was looking decent before I got out of the car. I was nearly to the front door when Alan's Celica came into full view. His backseat was jammed with balloons. A tangle of string attached a dozen cans to his bumper. Then the final brick crumbled: *Just Married* was scrawled in chalk across his back window.

"No," I said, frozen. How was this possible? It hadn't even been a *year*!

I caught movement behind the glass of the front door, which meant it was too late to turn around. I couldn't let them see me scurrying back to my car, speeding off in embarrassment. I forced a smile and walked the remaining few steps to the door. I hardly had time to knock before Alan swung it open.

"Hi," he said, surprised.

"Hi." After a moment, I added in a low voice, "You're *married*?"

He looked at the ground. "Yes, I am."

Over his shoulder, I saw a woman watching us. Thin, with long blond hair, she was older than I was but younger than Alan.

"Susan," he said, his voice falsely cheerful, "this is Carmen. She's an old friend of mine."

I smiled and extended my hand, trying not to cry. I was eighteen. How old a friend could I be? The tension was palpable, and the knowing, unsettled look in her eyes told me she felt it, too.

"It's nice to meet you, Carmen."

"You, too," I said. "And—congratulations. On the wedding, I mean."

"Thank you. Do you want to come in?"

"Oh. Sure."

I followed them into the kitchen, where Alan and I sat across from each other at the table. She stood beside him as we all chatted awkwardly for a few minutes. Then she touched his shoulder. "I'm just going to check on the heater. It's blowing pretty loudly."

"So," Alan said once she'd left. He drummed his fingers on the table. "You graduated from high school?"

"Yeah, last May."

"Are you still living at home?"

"No, I have my own apartment now."

He smiled. "That's good, Carmen. You were always so independent. So what are you doing now? Are you going to college?"

"No. I'm still working at Kathie and Bill's convenience store," I said. My heart was breaking. If he still had feelings for me, I couldn't tell. It didn't matter anyway. He was married, and we would never have another chance. "Well, listen," I said when Susan returned, "I'd better get going. It was real nice to see you. And nice to meet you, Susan."

I pushed my chair away from the table. I needed to get to my car before the tears forced their way out.

"It was good to see you, too, Carmen," Alan said. He

gave me a sad smile. "Take care of yourself, okay?"

"I will."

I hurried from the house as quickly as possible without outright running. Talking to him that day, smiling at his wife, pretending we had no history—it was the worst thing I'd ever had to do.

I thought of Alan often throughout my adult life. I never felt about anybody—even Herb—the way I had about him, and the memory of that first love lingered. Every so often, in different relationships, I wondered what would have happened if we'd gotten back together when he'd asked. Would we have gotten married one day? Or just broken up later down the line? When I was married to Herb, I tracked Alan down once or twice but never dared call him. He was married, and so was I. Memories were memories.

The Upper Valley is a small region, so Alan heard when I first got hurt. He mailed a letter to my father the week I came home, and Dad gave it to Kess a few months later. "This is from Alan," he said. "I didn't open it."

I had just been released from the hospital and was not prepared to hear what it said. "Kess, just put it away with all the other cards," I said. "One day I'll be able to read it. Dad, if he calls or anything, you can give him my number."

That never happened.

The letter remained unopened until I first regained sight in my right eye. I stumbled across it as I was sifting through the stacks of cards, and I held it with trembling hands. Then I took it to my magnifying glass.

The letter was typed and dated Saturday, November 24, 2007. It was addressed to my father:

Hello Joe,

I hope this letter finds you well and in good spirits. I heard the good news earlier this week that Carmen is coming home to Thetford for the holidays and that she was being released from the hospital in Boston. Please tell her I've been watching the news and following her progress right along since I first heard of her unbelievable circumstances. Also, our neighbors up here and the members of our little church here in East Hardwick are all extremely pleased that she is doing so well. Her progress has been watched by many with prayers and hope, and although much remains to yet get through, her progress has been amazing to many and also very much an inspiration. Without being intrusive in any way, Joe, I would like to be able to talk to Carm. Sometime alone, as time and circumstances might allow, perhaps on the phone or at home, wherever, under any means and circumstances that would allow her and you the most comfort with respect for her situation. I would certainly understand if this was not possible for some time in the distant future even and entertain no hope for visiting any time soon unless you feel it would be to her benefit. Please think about my request and get back to me at a time that might be convenient for you.

Very sincerely yours,

Alan

Below his note, Alan included a phone number and email address, but by the time I read it in 2009, the phone number was a dead end. Now, six months later, I was feeling a deep urge to contact him. It was different than when I had thought about him in the past; this was a *need* I couldn't explain. It weighed on me, and I pored over the letter again. All I could do was send an email to the address he'd provided and hope he occasionally checked it.

This is Carmen, I wrote. *Hope all is well. Please call me*, and I added my number.

As January turned to February with no reply, I noticed one section of my scars starting to swell. For ten days straight, the scars on my legs deepened to scarlet, as painful to look at as they felt to the touch. No lotion, balm, or pain medicine soothed them, and the inflammation made moving around even more difficult than usual. One of my doctors thought it might be because I had gained weight—I was finally approaching my typical one-thirty—and my skin was stretching. But I had gained the weight slowly, over a period of months, so the explanation didn't make sense to me. Then, as suddenly as the swelling began, it stopped—replaced by a new one the next day. The pattern continued for weeks: one section of scars flared up for seven to ten days, and as soon as it died down another continued the charge. My body was like a Christmas tree with broken lights.

"I'm just not sure what's causing this," said my doctor at Dartmouth-Hitchcock. While I couldn't see the expression in her eyes, her tone was genuinely puzzled. "I've never seen anything like it before."

"If we don't know what's causing the problem, how are we going to fix it?" I asked. I was desperate for the pain to stop.

"It could be because you're gaining weight and the skin is stretching. Keep doing what you're doing with your medication. Let's just keep an eye on it for now."

By March, Alan still hadn't responded to my email, but

my strange, fierce urge to see him hadn't faded. I called 4-1-1 a number of times to find him but had no luck. Day after day, as I suffered through the pain of my scars swelling, I tried to keep positive. Life would change. It would get better. There was a reason I hadn't been able to track Alan down, and there was a reason my scars were acting up this way. I had to believe that because otherwise, if this was all random and meaningless, I didn't know how I could go on.

On March 26, the day after Kess's birthday, I heard a news report that knocked the air from my chest. There was a missing kayaker, last seen in one of the landings for the Connecticut River, only two miles from my house. His body still hadn't surfaced. It was Alan.

The loss was immediate, choking. The only thing I could think to do was call my mother.

"Maybe it's not him," she tried to console me. "There are a lot of men with that name. Wait and see. It might not be him."

"It's him, Mom," I sobbed. "I know in my heart that it's him."

I spent the rest of that day and the next searching through my closet for old photos and letters. I found a photo album and notes he'd written me; his *I love you* made my body course with pain. I also came across an eight-by-ten photo that his friend Ray had taken. It was a picture of me taking a picture of Alan, sitting in the snow on top of a mountain. Icicles glinted from trees. The photo was creased and water damaged, and I felt a sharp pang of regret for not framing it when the images were clear and beautiful.

His body didn't surface for a month, during which

time I languished in grief. How was it possible that he was gone—that the day I saw him at eighteen would be the *last* time I'd see him? I had no sense of closure. What was the *purpose* of all this? The only thing that made sense to me now was my strong urge to see him. Perhaps it wasn't entirely dissimilar to when I had felt people's spirits changing, leaving, in the hospital. It was all wrapped up in my intuition, my little voice; maybe a part of me knew I *had* to see him because there was only limited time. That I missed my window was heartbreaking. I cried for hours each day, and the more distraught I became, the worse my scars flared up. Then, the more physical pain I was in, the less I was able to cope with my emotional despair. It was a crippling cycle. By April, I was the most depressed I had ever been.

One afternoon—and one afternoon only—I considered letting go. The whole winter and spring had been so difficult. Alan was dead. I didn't know whether my physical pain would ever ease. I spent my days sitting on the couch, listening to TV. This was no life. If it never improved, what was the point? I did not want this pain that surrounded me any longer. I wanted the peace and joy that would come with death. For the first time, I wondered if I was ready to end this struggle. Would my family understand?

I was home alone, crying and talking to myself out loud in the kitchen. My hands shook as I tried to pour a cup of coffee. "Can I hold on a little longer and see if it gets better?" I asked myself. I waited and listened, hoping for guidance one way or the other. "Why am I still here?"

In the end, it was the pain itself—so intolerable, so unimaginable—that brought me to a place of clarity: *I am more than just my pain.* I was a spirit having a human experience. I could find peace and joy without physical death. After all, I had made a *choice* to live, a choice that I remembered making. I had held on to find my place on earth. Yes, I had lost a lot. In fact, I had lost everything except the one thing I couldn't live without: my family. Life let me keep what I needed. What good would it do to dwell on everything else? I would just continue living depressed and dissatisfied, feeling sorry for myself for losing my sight, my face and body, and my independence. I hadn't done anything wrong, so why should I stay in this terrible dark place? No. I needed to consciously switch how I thought about what had happened to me—and what I was going to do with the rest of my life.

A few days after I hit bottom, I called my father. A lot of my conversations with family then involved venting about my pain and discomfort, but on this particular day I felt good. If I had chosen to be here, I should at least try to do something positive to reverse the negativity Herb had created—not just for me but for the world; what Herb had done was bad for the world.

"Dad," I said over the phone, "I think I'm starting to understand why this happened to me."

Dad showed his support through giving advice about practical matters, like finances. Though his anger was as fresh and raw as the day I was hurt, he was always willing to listen to me talk. "Why?" he asked.

"Maybe I was just taking one for the team," I said. "For humanity. Herb put all this negativity into the universe, right? Well, maybe I can top that with all the goodness I can put in. Maybe it's my *job* to start turning this cycle of violence around."

Dad listened thoughtfully. Then he said, "You've got

a lot on your plate."

"I know. But I think I can do it."

"Do you have a plan?"

"No," I said. "But I feel like I have the opportunity to change the world just by being me. By sharing my story and being honest, even when it hurts."

"So ... are you still thinking of writing a book?" he asked, somewhat warily.

"Absolutely. And when I'm feeling better, I'd also like to start speaking."

"That's a lot to take on," he said again. "Are you sure you're ready for it?"

"Physically? No. Not at all. But I'll get there."

In May, just one month after I thought about giving up, life started turning around. Dr. Pomahac, my surgeon at Brigham, told me about a surgery he wanted to do to eliminate the scar tissue on my neck. Besides the groupings of scars that were still swelling, my neck gave me the most trouble. The scars were banded so tightly that they pulled my head forward, making it immensely difficult to do simple tasks like speaking clearly and eating without drooling. The surgery was extreme: it would require Dr. Pomahac to place a tissue expander in my back, which he would inflate a little more every week throughout the summer. By early fall, my tissue should have stretched enough for him to excise it and use it to replace the extensive scarring on my neck. Since it was my own tissue, there was no risk of rejection.

"What are the chances the surgery will relieve my neck discomfort?" I asked.

Dr. Pomahac said, "There is a ninety-six percent chance that your neck won't give you problems again."

"Ninety-six percent?" I exclaimed, swept up in his optimism. "Well, that's great—let's do it!"

I called Adam Sullivan, a local TV reporter who had done a story on me in the past, and asked if he would be interested in doing an update. For the first time in a long time, I was excited to talk about my future. Adam was glad to hear from me and came over to interview me for the segment. By now, I was comfortable with the media, though I still refused to talk about what happened that night. I was waiting to share it in my book.

At first, I talked my story out into a tape recorder. I tried to put my thoughts together in some cohesive fashion. Where should I start the book? With the attack? Earlier, with my background, or somewhere in the middle, when I met Herb? I decided to start with the latter. At the end of May, near my forty-second birthday, I picked up a pen.

Writing was a physically daunting task. I wrote slower than I had before and lost energy quickly. I recognized how overwhelming a project this would be, but I had to try. Over what felt like hours, I penned my first sentence: *No one could have convinced me that my life would take such a dramatic turn*. After that, the first chapter came fairly easily. I talked about my background in the Upper Valley, moving out to LA, meeting Herb. When I hit Chapter 2, I stalled; this was where I would write about what happened.

"You can do this, Carm," I coached myself. "You want to share your story. It can help people."

Alone at my magnifying machine, I felt physically ill with what I was doing. The experience of reliving that night, trying to capture each detail as vividly as I remembered it, was sickening. Halfway through, I let my pen drop and rushed to my bedroom, the edges of my limited vision blackening.

It took two full days to write the story of what Herb did. Writing it was so different from simply thinking about it. Now that it was on paper, it seemed so … permanent, as if I were sending my story into the world with no power to retract it and no control over the effect it would have on those who read it. It was scary but exactly what I wanted. As I approached the three-year anniversary of the attack, I could sense the road changing beneath my feet. My path was becoming clear.

CHAPTER 17

GREATEST GIFT

BY SUMMER OF 2010, I HAD BEEN AT MY LOWEST, only to emerge stronger and more optimistic than ever before. When you are truly tired of something negative in your life, lasting change can occur. But that doesn't seem to happen often. Perhaps it's because we are so good at burying our negative feelings; if they don't come to the surface and slap us in the face, we don't do anything about them. I had been slapped. I didn't want to just "live with" what had happened. I didn't want to just "survive." Why should *I* crumple under the weight of what Herb did? I didn't have to be damaged because of his actions. If I got sucked into that negativity, he won.

The win/lose mentality was what I needed back then to fuel me forward. I needed to win on my own terms, for myself. Herb would never hurt me again, and I was free to *choose* how I moved forward from here. I didn't have to focus on loss. I didn't have to succumb to how our society treats disabled people, as burdensome creatures who can no longer contribute productively. I didn't choose to stay for that. I chose to stay for something big. People might say that was wishful thinking—and it was. Everything big starts with desire. You create the reality as time goes on.

Here was my reality: I wasn't going to be a nurse again. For that matter, I wasn't going to be any organization's typical employee. That admission was scary at first, since I had my girls to think about, but it forced me to think about goals. The whole time I'd been hurt, I'd felt the importance of sharing my story; that was why I'd connected with the media early on and why I continued to build those relationships. Speaking in public wasn't that far a stretch. Except for talking about that night, I was open to discussing what had happened and what I was slowly learning. Could I make a career out of it?

At this point, I'd been trying to write my book for several weeks and had to face facts: doing it myself would be next to impossible. Simply paying my bills was a half-hour endeavor in front of my magnifying machine, and I had to sit down for hours afterwards to recoup my strength. Writing was worse. I could only manage ten or fifteen minutes at a time before my back, neck, and arms throbbed and cramped. At this rate, I'd be a hundred years old by the time my book was finished. There had to be other options, and I was determined to explore each one.

In June, I was temporarily distracted from thoughts of my new path by my tissue-expander surgery. Dr. Pomahac inserted an inflatable balloon device about the size of a liter bag beneath the skin of the right side of my back. After I woke up in the recovery room, Dr. Pomahac came in to brief me on the operation.

"Everything went well with the tissue expander," he said. "But we noticed something strange. All that redness and swelling on your leg—it went away when we put you under."

"Why would it do that?" I asked.

"I don't know, but we practically watched it go away. In any case, I'll see you next month to evaluate how you're doing with the tissue expander."

On the drive ride back to Lebanon three days later, what Dr. Pomahac had said about my scars nagged at me. Why would the anesthesia make them disappear? Could it be that they faded once my *mind* was at rest? Could they actually be a physical manifestation of my emotional struggles? If that was true, I was the only one with the power to heal myself. But how?

Once I had recovered from the surgery enough to go out, I asked my mother to take me to the bookstore.

"What do you want to do there?" she asked curiously.

"There's so much knowledge out there," I said. "Surely there's *something* that will help me figure out how to move forward."

"What do you mean?"

"I may not be able to do much physically, but I can still work on myself."

In the past, I had always turned to self-help books when I needed to shift my line of thought. My bookshelf in Hawthorne was full of books I'd picked up when I felt stunted. I remembered reading one called *Getting Unstuck* after moving to LA. I enjoyed reading it, feeling as though my urge for something more wasn't crazy. Still, as inspired as I felt in the moment, I had never taken the time to fully work on my self-development. Not many people do. Now, at the cusp of what I felt would be a new stage in my journey—perhaps that very same *something more*—it seemed crucial. Besides, I was *bored*. If I was going to sit around the house all day with a big lump on my back, the least I could do was stimulate my mind and see what happened.

The comforting smell of paper and coffee greeted us when we walked into the bookstore in West Lebanon. I couldn't read print books anymore, so my mother and I wandered into the audio books section. She stood next to me looking at the titles, a finger moving from one to the next.

"Do you know which one you want?" she asked.

"No. Can you just read the titles to me?"

Mom slowly read out the titles and authors of the audio books. They all sounded similar until one caught my attention.

"*Embracing Change*, by Louise Hay," Mom read.

"Stop," I said. "What was that title again?"

"*Embracing Change.*"

I was imbued with the same sense of optimism I'd felt in the past, picking up a book that promised to help me improve my life. Embracing change sounded exactly like what I needed to do. "Let's get that one," I said.

Back home in my bedroom, I slid the CD into the player Herb had given me for Christmas in 1998. It was all beat up, covered in paint from the times I'd used it while painting the kids' rooms, but I knew where the buttons were and that I could rely on it. It was the only thing Herb had given me that I still owned.

With the CD in the player, I sat in my rocking chair and rested my feet on the TV stand. I pushed myself back and forth as a woman's voice filled the room.

I didn't know who Louise Hay was when I bought the book, but her message immediately resonated with me. She explained how she'd been horribly abused as a child and, despite a good education and career, had never fully dealt with it. Later, when she was in her fifties, she was diagnosed with cancer. She believed the cancer was a symptom, a "dis-ease." Negativity was the disease. Rather than go through radiation and chemotherapy—traditional treatments—she set about healing herself with affirmations, visualization, prayer, therapy, and healthy eating. She released her negativity and emotional trauma, and—shocking everyone—she went into remission. Now she was well into her eighties and the cancer had never returned. Such, she said, was the power of the mind.

Louise Hay was the first "new age" author I listened to, and her personal story was more inspiring to me than anything else was. I didn't have a disease, but I *was* injured. If I could heal my heart from its emotional and psychological burdens, become happy and comfortable with myself, maybe my physical healing would come.

Quietly, I went on a quest. I bought audio book after audio book—Deepak Chopra, Dr. Wayne Dyer, Tony Robbins—and listened to them in the peaceful solitude of my bedroom. The messages fueled me the way people are inspired after going to conferences or motivational speeches. But, unlike those people who return to normal lives—going to work, raising a family, cooking dinner—and soon forget their moments of conviction, I had nothing else to do but incorporate these messages into my life. Focus was key!

One of the things that stuck out to me from *Embracing Change* was the idea of forgiveness. When Louise Hay got cancer, she realized she had never forgiven her abuser for what he had done to her as a child, and she claimed this was a huge source of her negativity. "Forgiveness isn't something we do for others," she reminded the listener.

"It's something we do for ourselves."

Forgiveness. There was that word again. I didn't hate Herb. I didn't think vengeful thoughts. After the first couple of years, when I thought of the million ways I could have changed the outcome of the attack, I hardly thought of him at all. But forgiveness hadn't even been on my radar until George mentioned it in his last visit. I hadn't forgiven Herb, and I didn't know if I could. I didn't know if I *should.* To forgive someone for something as shattering as what Herb did makes you feel as though you are condoning his actions, absolving him from the pain he caused. But was that the truth? Or was Louise Hay right, with that old cliché of forgiveness being something we do for ourselves?

If that was true, I wondered whether *not* forgiving Herb was blocking me from the things I wanted to do. I wanted to start speaking to people about what had happened. So many survivors don't do that. Unless I'm in the burn unit of Brigham, even I don't see people like me out there. We're hurt and burned and scarred, and we hide. I didn't want to hide, but I also didn't want my story to *depress* people! And I suspected it would if I tried to start speaking. I needed to reach the next level of understanding about why this had happened—needed to be totally comfortable with *me.* That motivated me to at least think about forgiveness, what it meant in the context of my life.

So—what were the implications of *not* forgiving Herb? He wanted to hurt people. He wanted everyone who loved me to feel pain. He wanted negativity. If I didn't forgive him, did that mean he won because the negativity remained in my own mind? And what about what Dr. Pomahac had said about my scars tempering when I was under anesthesia? Was it possible that the inflammation was a "symptom," as Louise Hay would call it, of the negativity caused by not forgiving? It seemed as though the least I could do, if I truly wanted to reverse the bad Herb had put into the world, was try.

When you embark on a mission without being attached to the outcome, you are released of the burden of expectation. Louise Hay calls this "letting go and allowing." So when I thought about trying to forgive Herb, I didn't expect to succeed. At least not right away. I wasn't even sure how to go about forgiveness. Was it a yes/no decision? A process? Would I know if I *had* forgiven him?

"Okay," I said to myself, breathing deeply. "You had a lot of good years together. Remember the time he got you the sun and moon mirror that you saw in the window of the shop and loved? You told him about it and he went back and bought it."

Herb was always good with gifts. Like most men, he hated shopping, but he always made it a point to buy me something I said I wanted, whether I asked for it as a birthday gift or just mentioned it in passing. He liked making me happy.

"Remember his laugh?" I asked myself. I knew now, of course, that Herb had been deeply unhappy, but there had been days when he was jolly, when he laughed and was silly and wrapped his arms around me in bed. It was hard, this compartmentalization between what he had done and who he had been, but a little bit at a time I forced myself to remember the good. I didn't know if I was on my way to forgiving, but it felt like a good place to start.

While I worked on forgiving Herb, I also went to weekly appointments at Dartmouth-Hitchcock. Each time, a doctor injected the tissue expander with saline, and I followed up once a month with Dr. Pomahac. Slowly, the device expanded to the size of a small loaf of bread. It was hugely uncomfortable, and I took large amounts of painkillers to get through the process. I kept reminding myself that this was temporary and that after the surgery, my neck problems would only be a memory. I never doubted that the surgery would work.

The weeks passed, and I lay low. One of the few things I did, besides listen to my audio books, was go out to dinner on the afternoons of my doctors' appointments. My mother had started dating a man named Marshall, with whom she'd gone to high school, and the three of us were fixtures at local restaurants. Marshall was shy about meeting me at first. Like most people in the Upper Valley, he had heard of me. My mother would stop by to bring me groceries and then hurry off, saying, "Marshall's in the car!" After this happened a couple of times, I asked to go out and meet him.

"It's not like he's going to come inside and meet me!" I said.

I followed my mother outside, and Marshall got out of the car. He was a big man, six feet tall and two hundred pounds, but his hand was gentle when he shook mine. "It's good to finally meet you," he said.

After that, the three of us went to dinner regularly.

Aside from that, I was home alone for most of the summer. Liza had just graduated high school and both girls were working, so I spent my time losing—then finding—myself in audio books. I listened to books on Buddhism and Dalism, the law of attraction and the idea of manifesting your own life. I was compelled by books that tried, in a non-religious way, to figure out why we're here. Again and again, I came back to the idea that life is a choice. Everything *about* life is a choice … including forgiveness.

The more I thought about forgiveness as a *choice*, the more I was forced to contemplate my other choices. Slowly, I was becoming more intentional about what I said and more analytical about how I felt. I tried to be careful about what I told my kids, because I didn't want them to think life had to be hard; it doesn't have to be hard. "Don't listen to the 'you have to's,'" I said. "There's no pre-set course that you *have to* take. You put your effort in where you want to put your effort in." I stopped snapping at them for making age-appropriate mistakes like getting speeding tickets or not picking up after themselves. I could imagine people thinking I let my kids run all over me, but I didn't. They were teenagers, on their way to becoming adults. I simply let them live their lives.

The most important message I started relaying to Liza and Hannah was to be selfish—to take care of themselves first and not to compromise. I didn't mean that they shouldn't empathize with others or that they should insist on their way at the detriment of someone else's wellbeing. I meant they shouldn't go to college because *I* wanted them to go to college. They shouldn't live somewhere because they thought *I* wanted them to. I wanted them to make their own decisions and own them. The first question I asked when they told me of any choice they made was, "Is that what *you* want?" If I had any influence at all over my girls, I hoped it would be to instill the importance of finding their own happiness. They could attract good things to themselves—we all can—but they *had to* be happy first.

With such a focus on happiness, I launched into self-examination: where and toward whom was I feeling negative at any given time? Most importantly, why? There were times I caught myself feeling passive-aggressive toward Kess for no reason I could immediately name. The more I thought about it, the more I realized it was old sister stuff: she didn't come see me when I wanted her to; she didn't include me in her life when I wanted to be. These were resentments I didn't even know I had! I thought, *I haven't forgiven her for that?* Here I was, trying to forgive Herb, and I hadn't forgiven my sister for hurting my feelings a decade ago.

My attempts to forgive Herb led me to release the negativity I held toward others, and the more negativity I released, the more I was able to think kindly of Herb. Once, I was watching a football game and, without meaning to, I thought of him. We used to watch football all winter long, cuddled up together and yelling at the TV. I remembered teasing him, saying the only reason he married me was because I loved the game as much as he did. The thought made me smile.

Herb was paying his debt to society. He didn't have the freedom I had and couldn't make the choices I could make. What I was starting to realize was that he hadn't taken anything away from me; he had *added* to me, the hard way.

After all of my self-reflection, meditation, and work to forgive Herb, I concluded that if he could live it over again, he would choose not to hurt me. But he had, and now I needed to move forward.

I realized, as I tried to forgive Herb, that I was doing it for me. And once I realized that, I was happy with the way I'd chosen to forgive. I felt as though I were a relationship archaeologist, sifting through the rubble in my heart and taking a brush to the pieces of our good times that I found. I could set them on a shelf in my mind, one right next to the other, and look at them when I needed to remember that *this*—what he'd done—wasn't who he was; that I couldn't have known it was coming; and that we had been happy once. This didn't mean I condoned what he had done. Of course not. I didn't deserve it. I was starting to believe, however, that there must be a part of my spirit that was willing to endure this in order to grow and help people. That was why I did not fear him, nor could I find any significant signs that he would "lose it," as he said.

Did I come into this current life of mine willingly, aware of what was to happen? If the answer was yes, then what did that mean? Was my true calling intertwined with all the sadness, pain, violence, and rage in the world? It must be, because I could survive and look toward climbing the next peak in my life. Of course, I did not want such violence in my life again. How could I make sure it never came? One way, I thought, was to reach for peace, love, and joy and to know that my tragedy could help others along the way.

As a starting point, I called my therapist and asked if I could speak to the medical students at Dartmouth-Hitchcock. I hadn't seen her in a year, but I thought med students could benefit from listening to a patient like me, and it would help me figure out whether I was actually ready to speak.

In August, when my tissue expander was the size of a brick protruding from my back, I went to talk to the students. My mother drove me to Dartmouth-Hitchcock, and we made our way to a small conference room filled with a dozen third- and fourth-year students. My vision was steady at 20/400, so while I couldn't distinguish facial expressions, I could see the group sitting in a circle. They seemed young to me, in their early to mid-twenties, and they were respectfully silent as I spoke. Keeping in mind that they were medical students, I stayed focused on my injuries and surgeries: I recounted all my skin grafts and corneal transplants, and I explained that the lump on my back was a tissue expander that Dr. Pomahac felt sure would cure me of my neck problems. Afterward, I opened the floor to questions.

"How many more surgeries will you need?" one student asked.

"I hope not very many. The scars on my neck give me the most trouble, and the tissue expander surgery should correct those."

"How have your daughters coped?" another student asked.

"They've always done well," I said. "They went to counseling for the first six months, but after that it was life as usual. They're normal kids. They get in trouble now and again, but I don't worry that it's because of what happened. It's because they're teenagers!"

The students laughed.

My mother was in the room, and one student asked her how difficult this experience had been for her. She cried a little as she told them how hard the last three years had been, and I cried a little, too. I didn't berate myself for becoming emotional, since this was my first time speaking, and I knew I would only get stronger.

I felt good after the talk—reinvigorated. I spoke to the doctor in charge of this rotation, and we agreed that I would come speak every six or seven weeks to a new crop of medical students. In between, I would continue listening to my audio books and developing my speaking focus. As much as I wanted to educate the students, I also wanted to inspire. I wanted to show that forgiveness could be found, even in the worst of pain and betrayal. Had I forgiven? I wasn't sure how to tell, but something in me felt better, lighter. And by September, it had been months since my scars had flared up. It couldn't be a coincidence.

CHAPTER 18

PHOENIX

AFTER A LONG SUMMER OF LIVING WITH THE TISSUE expander, I had surgery on Tuesday, September 14. Dr. Pomahac and his team cut me from my armpit to my hip in order to remove the device, which was bloated with about forty-seven ounces of saline. Then they excised as much of my stretched skin and tissue as they could to replace the scars on my neck. It was a long, painful surgery, but I was back home by Friday.

I'd lost the discomfort of the tissue expander but gained something worse: a wooden contraption that he sewed below my ears and on both sides of my neck to keep the skin and tissue stretched out. My chin rested on a pad of sheepskin wool. It was as if I had grown a solid, bulky beard. Every movement felt unnatural and eating was almost impossible. Food kept catching and collecting beneath it, inevitably causing terrible discomfort.

"It's worth it, Carm," I told myself. "If the surgery works like he said it would, if it makes your neck better, it's worth it."

Ten days later, it was clear I had an infection—and a bad one at that. Whatever pain I might feel without the contraption had to be more bearable than with it, so I went back to the hospital to have it removed. The relief was immediate, though the infection would take some

217

time to heal.

The next week, I returned to Brigham to have one hundred thirty stitches removed from my sides. My skin was so sensitive from being burned—I only had two or three layers, whereas most people had eleven—that the pain was exponentially greater than it would be for non-burn patients. But again, if Dr. Pomahac was right and there was a ninety-six percent chance my neck would no longer cause so much suffering, this was all worth it.

I was supposed to see improvement immediately, and I did feel better for the first six weeks. Then, slowly, my neck began tightening again. When I touched it with my fingers, I could feel that the scars were starting to bulge. Then the infection under my chin grew some scar band of its own. "Wait and see," I told myself. "It's still too soon to tell."

The next month provided something of a distraction. My friend George from the Phoenix Society had invited me to that year's World Burn Conference in Galveston, Texas. The conference drew somewhere around a thousand burn survivors and their families. It lasted for several days, with dozens of different events, sessions, and panels. I was particularly interested in the keynote speakers. They were helping people by sharing their stories, as I felt I could help people with mine. There was a lot I could learn by attending.

The travel day was going to be long. On a Wednesday, Mom and I took a morning bus from West Lebanon to Boston, where we would fly into Houston and then board another bus to Galveston. It my first time flying since being injured, and though I knew I wasn't allowed more than several ounces of liquids or creams, I took my enormous Eucerin bottle in my carry-on; the plane air would dry out my scars like nothing else.

"I'm sorry, ma'am," said a security employee. "You can't take more than three point four ounces on the plane."

"Are you kidding me?" I said. "It's just lotion. I need it for medical reasons."

The employee looked at me. I was clearly disfigured, with a bandage still wrapped around an open wound on the back of my head.

"We'll need to test the cream, ma'am," he said.

Mom and I waited fifteen minutes while they took the bottle of Eucerin to make sure it was, in fact, just lotion. Then they returned the bottle to me for the flight.

It was five o'clock when we arrived in Galveston. The October afternoon was sunny and breezy, with a salty tang in the air. I wanted to enjoy the balmy weather but was so uncomfortable that we went straight to the hotel. The incisions from my surgery stung, and my limited eyesight made me more tired than I should be at that time of day. As much as I wanted to meet some of the other conference attendees, all I could do was lie down.

"Are you feeling okay, Carm?" Mom asked.

"No, I'm not," I snapped. "I'm really uncomfortable. I thought I was supposed to feel better by now."

I was taking out my exhaustion and frustration on her, I knew, but I couldn't keep it to myself. I wasn't feeling as well as I wanted, and I wasn't accepting that yet. Mom never got defensive when I was irritable. She always tried to be supportive. The hardest thing for her was to know I was hurting when she could do nothing to make me feel better.

"Well," she said quietly, "let's get some rest and see how

you do tomorrow."

The next day, Mom and I went to see one of the keynote speakers. His name was Dan Caro, and he'd lost his hands from being burned as a little boy. He called himself "No-Hands Dan." He was a drummer.

Before a full, rapt audience, Dan talked about getting burned so young and what it had been like to grow up without hands. He told us about the triumph of being able to tie his shoes for the first time. Then he played the drums. It was an exuberant beat that got everybody pumped, and I remembered seeing him on PBS the week before. I had told Kess, "I saw this burn guy on TV today—he was playing drums with no hands." Kess responded, "Yeah, that's the guy who's going to be at World Burn." By the time I saw him speak and play, I felt as if I were seeing a celebrity. Even better, I was seeing someone doing what I wanted to do: fill others with the drumbeat of conviction that anything was possible and that our scars need only remind us of what we've learned—not limit where we're going.

Regardless of my discomfort, there was one session I was determined to attend: "Forgiveness." It was held specifically for people who were burned by others, and I wanted to go alone. I thought the discussions might be too heavy for my mother, too raw. She didn't need to revisit the cause of my injuries or examine how completely she'd forgiven Herb, nor did I think she'd want to hear painful stories from other burn victims.

"Mom, I think I'm just going to handle this one on my own," I said to her over lunch. We were sitting in an enormous, cafeteria-style room, with big round tables and hundreds of people talking over one another. "Is that all right with you?"

Mom nodded across the table. Though I couldn't make out specific facial expressions, I thought she might be relieved. "I don't think I want to go to that anyway," she said. "It doesn't feel appropriate."

Mom consulted the schedule, and she helped me find my way to the big, bright room where the session would be held. The hotel was huge and labyrinthine, and we were constantly asking people for directions. We separated at the door, and Mom told me she'd be waiting outside when the session let out. I assumed she'd spend the next hour talking to Marshall on the phone. I waved good-bye and walked to a group of folding chairs. Light poured in from one side of the room; perhaps one wall was all windows.

In the minutes before the session began, thirty or forty people filled the seats around me. Most of them were women, but there were a handful of men as well. The murmur in the room quieted as the leader of the session addressed the group. She was a minister of some kind, and her voice was low and calm as she spoke.

"I want to give you all space to share how you feel," she said. "This is a place for us to explore forgiveness, not to feel forced into it. Now, I'd like to invite anyone who wants to speak to introduce themselves. And if you're comfortable, please share a little bit of your story."

Without sight, I had become sensitive to tone; I could tell as soon as someone started speaking whether they had forgiven or not. One man had been electrocuted by two other men. His tone was weighty and sad, as if he'd resigned himself to his life. He hadn't forgiven. One woman wouldn't say the details of how she'd been burned. Her voice was like a wire stretched taut, on the verge of snapping with anger. She hadn't forgiven, either.

I couldn't help wondering who among these people was disfigured, like me, and who had "hidden burns." There were hundreds of people at the conference who, like my friend George, didn't look injured. Their wounds were concealed beneath light linen shirts, loose dresses, or blue jeans. That group, I learned, struggled with different issues because of their ability to hide their injuries; hiding them meant they didn't necessarily need to tell people their story. I imagined that deciding whom to tell, and when, must be difficult. It would be tempting to simply pretend the wounds didn't exist, but I suspected the longer they went without sharing their stories, the less they were actually able to move forward. Disfigured survivors didn't have a choice. They could either open themselves to the questions and curiosity, or they could hide away. To me, of course, the choice was obvious.

Throughout the session, I kept piping up with positive words. I hadn't planned on saying anything, but I wanted to know if I'd forgiven. If I could talk about it as if I had and it felt truthful, then I would have my answer. If I couldn't talk about it, if it turned out I hadn't forgiven, it didn't matter. No one knew me here. No one was going to judge.

"You know," I ventured, "forgiveness is about helping ourselves, not the people who hurt us."

I smiled to myself, remembering how much I'd wanted to understand what those words meant the first time I heard Louise Hay speak them.

"If you want to forgive, if you can see that the advantages to it are to *you*," I continued, "then the thing to know is that forgiveness is letting go. I think people in our situation have a hard time letting go because of the way it happened. But for me, the way it happened made it easier."

"Can you explain what you mean by that?" the minister asked.

I turned my head toward the light-filled side of the room. "Well, if I had been a battered wife and he had done this, would I be blaming myself for staying, year after year? I think a lot of women blame themselves because they didn't leave, and that makes forgiveness harder because they feel a need to forgive themselves, too. And that's just one situation. I'm sure I would have a hard time looking in the mirror if I felt I had caused this in some way. But we can't take responsibility for someone else's actions. We just can't. I take responsibility for myself but never for him. Never for what he did. There is no self-blame here."

Quickly, unbidden, came a flash of that night. Liza's room, my hands tied. As soon as I was bound, I realized, there was nothing I could do to prevent what came. It was not my responsibility.

"No one in this room should blame themselves, no matter what their situation," I said.

This was the first time I'd spoken to a room of people who had been in similar situations. It was different than answering questions for reporters or speaking to the medical students. It was just us here, and I felt good about what I had said. That was when I realized the startling truth: I must have forgiven Herb. Somehow, my efforts over the summer had worked. I didn't think it could have been that easy, but it was. I was no longer angry or bitter. I might not have been the best at accepting when I didn't feel as well as I wanted, but I accepted what happened. It was no longer a nightmare from which I kept hoping to wake. It was simply my life.

At the end of the hour-long session, the woman next

to me leaned close. "You are really brave," she said softly. "Really. You are so courageous for saying what you said."

From my other side came the minister's voice. "Thank you for your input," she said. "You are very inspiring for those who haven't forgiven. You are an example of the good that can come in your own heart from moving forward in this way."

I was taken aback by the praise, but I basked in it. It seemed like further confirmation that, after three years of stumbling through thorny brush, I had found my way into a clearing. I had forgiven.

○ ○ ○

Later that day, something special happened at the conference: a wedding ceremony.

My friend Melisa and her boyfriend Erin wanted to get married at World Burn, because that was where they'd met in 2005. Melisa was a ninety-five percent burn survivor. Her ex-husband—who had been emotionally but not physically abusive—poured gas over her after she told him she wanted a divorce. She was holding a lit cigarette, and within seconds her whole body was in flames. She was burned everywhere, and her recovery was long and excruciating. I knew less about Erin, though I knew he had gotten caught in a building fire. They fell in love at a time of their lives when they thought romantic relationships were a lost option.

Poetically, Melisa and Erin were married at a fire station in Galveston. There were tables and chairs set out in the garage, and a cool ocean breeze swept in from the coast. The ceremony was small, with about thirty people attending. There were a lot of couples, including some in which only one partner was burned. I sat in back with my mother. I couldn't hear much over the crackly speaker system, but I could feel the love and joy. I thought, *If this is something I want in my future, I can have it.*

Physically and emotionally, I was far from being able to have a relationship. But knowing that Melisa and Erin had found each other, that other burn survivors fell in love and got married, made me optimistic. The man I was with could not be an average Joe, of course. He would have to see my inner beauty, as my outer beauty had been replaced with scar tissue and discolored skin. He would need to be as strong and as sensitive as me, and outwardly joyous and loving, making me laugh. As for the physical components, I was burned everywhere; how would I show someone my body? When and how would I be able to tolerate sex? *Someday,* I thought. *Someday.*

What I *didn't* worry about when I considered future relationships was the possibility of someone hurting me again. While not infallible, my intuition had been honed; I read people better now than I ever had. If I saw any red flags, even those as minor as the ones that had been there with Herb, I would move on. But the main reason I didn't worry was because I was convinced that my attack was an isolated incident. It had happened for a reason that I was already discovering; I would not need to be hurt again in order to learn those lessons. From here on out, I was almost positive I would not attract anyone violent into my life.

I left World Burn the next day feeling as though the purpose I had uncovered that summer was its own flame, building heat within me. In the best way possible, I no longer felt as though I had a choice about my future:

I had to use what happened to me to help others. Even if my recovery was far from over, I was ready to begin the next phase of my journey.

CHAPTER 19

FREEDOM

AFTER GALVESTON, I FELT A RESTLESS STIRRING TO push myself further. There had been so many people at World Burn—like Melisa and Erin—whose recovery was far ahead of mine. I wanted to be one of them. I wanted to be an example of someone living her life, not just thinking about it.

My friend Eileen, from LA, had recently moved to New Jersey to take care of her mother. Both of her parents had gotten sick in 2006, and her father passed away a couple of years later. She had emailed my sister earlier that summer, and Kess passed her phone number to me. So much had happened since California—I had lost so many friends—that I didn't know if I wanted to reconnect. It wasn't worth it to me if she would eventually slide from my life again. When I finally called her, I told her the truth: that it was too emotional to re-establish a friendship if it wasn't going to last. It may not have been fair, but I gave her an ultimatum.

"If you say you want to be friends, then I want you in my life," I said. "If you can't handle that, I'd rather not even try."

She said, "I will be here for you."

Eileen often traveled to Stamford, Connecticut, to stay with her sister Mary Anne. Stamford was a six-and-a-half-hour train ride from White River, Vermont, and I suggested that I go out to visit. I was ready to do something by myself.

"I'd love that!" Eileen said.

I called the train station to buy my ticket in advance and told them I was legally blind; I would need help getting off the train at the right stop. They made sure everything was taken care of, and I spent most of that ride dozing and listening to CDs on my portable CD player. When the train stopped in Stamford, night had already fallen.

A train employee helped me down onto the station, and I felt only a moment of uncertainty before hearing my name: "Carmen!" a woman called. "Carmen, it's Patty, Eileen's sister! Eileen, she's over here!"

I walked toward Patty's voice, and she soon took my arm. I heard hurried footsteps in our direction and then caught movement before my eye.

"Oh, Carmen," Eileen said, "you look great. I'm so glad you made it."

She hugged me, and I breathed a sigh of relief that Eileen had reacted so well to seeing me. Then again, I wasn't surprised. Eileen had been a supervisor and nurse educator at UCLA, and I was a charge nurse beneath her. Tough and understanding, she was mature and able to deal with a floor that was never quiet, never still. I admired her because she never flinched at the frantic activity and always did her best—not just good enough. Though we'd never spent time together outside the hospital, reuniting now felt natural and happy.

It was early evening, and as we walked to their car, Eileen asked me what I'd like to do that night.

Ruefully, I said, "To be honest, I'm ready for bed."

Eileen laughed and patted my shoulder. "We'll get a good night's rest and catch up more tomorrow."

° ° °

Over the next few days, Eileen's sister's house was alive with activity. Mary Anne was divorced, with a daughter named Michaela who lived downstairs while she went to graduate school. Eileen's other sisters—Patty, Elizabeth, and Katie—all stopped by at different times with their kids, and their mom was alert and clear even though she had a tracheotomy. Everybody was in each other's business, laughing, talking, and telling old teasing stories. It was obvious that they actually *liked* one another. I sensed that all five sisters had been there for each other over the years—defending, protecting, and scolding when the times called for it. Their energy made the house warm and welcoming. I hadn't laughed so much in years.

Because I still couldn't do much physically, we mostly sat around the house and talked. But Eileen and I also took several walks around the neighborhood. It was a quiet suburb, with wide paved roads and not a lot of traffic. We were able to walk leisurely, with Eileen's leashed dog running ahead and impatiently circling back around her legs.

On one of our walks, I told Eileen about the dreams I had while I was in the coma. She was fascinated, especially with my "life is a choice" dream. I think she felt there was something magical about the mystery of life being revealed to me in some way. It made her think about why we were all here, what our purposes were, and who had designed them.

"I wonder who you were listening to," she said, her voice hushed and awed.

When we got back to the house, she wasted no time before corralling her sisters and Michaela into the kitchen. "Carmen just told me the most amazing story," she said. "Tell them, Carmen!"

We sat around the table, and I repeated what I remembered about the dream: the different doors, the disembodied voice, the ball of dust, the movie screen. Life is a choice. When I finished, the room was silent.

"Oh, my God," Patty breathed.

"I know," Eileen said. "I know."

They were so genuinely moved that I felt giddy. I wanted to tell them of my plan to speak and write, though I was scared that I hadn't done enough work to speak without being depressing. I needed to be able to say I was feeling good and that my life was better now than it had been; I was getting there, but I knew I hadn't reached that point completely.

Hesitantly, I said, "You know … I've started to write a book. It's slow going, but I'm trying. I've also looked into ghostwriting. And I'm thinking about starting to speak in public about what I've learned through all this."

Only a beat passed before the room exploded with enthusiasm.

"Carmen, yes! That makes so much sense. I mean, how can you not?" Eileen shrieked.

Patty agreed. "Just listening to you, the way you look at the world—it's so inspiring."

"Really?" I laughed. "You don't think it would just depress people?"

They laughed, too. Then Eileen said, more seriously, "Carm, you can help so many more people now than you ever could as a nurse. Especially women. We could all stand to be more aware of our choices and to look out for signs that we're on the wrong path. And for people who have been hurt like you—they need to know it's not the end."

I didn't need to see their faces to feel how enthusiastic, how sincere, their support was. I had been planning to wait on speaking until I felt significantly better, but Eileen was right. This was my opportunity to help others in an entirely different way. Why wait if I could start now?

I hoped they could sense how widely I was smiling inside.

○ ○ ○

Once I returned from my trip, I wrote almost every day. Between ten and eleven o'clock, I sat at the granite-top desk in the living room. I slid my paper beneath the lens of my magnifying machine so I could see words as I penned them, laying each page face down on the desk as I finished. Eileen's niece, Michaela, had offered to type it all up for me, and I slowly assembled a pile that I would send to her after Christmas. Then I shifted my focus to speaking.

The first group I called was WISE, a non-profit domestic violence advocacy organization in the Upper Valley. I told the event coordinator that I was going to start speaking in the near future.

"That's great!" she said. "We have a fortieth anniversary event in the spring. I'd love to keep you in mind for that."

"That would be perfect," I said. I hung up feeling eager and excited, like a child with something to look forward to.

After that, I remembered the medical students. I had phoned the doctor at the end of September, leaving a message that I was ready to speak again, and he hadn't returned my call. This time he answered.

"Hi, it's Carmen," I said. "I just wanted to let you know that I'm available to speak to the next group of students whenever you're ready."

To my surprise, there was a long silence on the line.

"I'm sorry I haven't called you," he said. "I talked to your therapist, and she felt it was too difficult for you."

"What?" I said. "You talked to my therapist? But I'm good. I'd really like to go back and speak."

"Well," he said, stuttering slightly, "I don't have anything scheduled. Nothing's going to happen before the holidays. Let me see if I can get something for you in January."

"Please let me know," I said. "I really want to talk to those students, and I'm more than available."

I knew he wasn't going to call me back, and I felt betrayed. I'd seen my therapist a few times after speaking with the medical students, and while I probably cried about my general discomfort—as I usually did to release negativity—I never said speaking was too difficult or that I didn't want to do it again. While she was right to be concerned, because she cared, she should have come directly to me with her worries. I wouldn't have dismissed them, but neither would I have let them deter me from my path. I deserved some creative control over my life.

Fine, I thought, exhaling loudly. These were their choices, not mine. Unfortunately, it was the medical students who would lose out. I would move on to the next opportunity.

Over the holidays, I received a card from an elderly lady who was a friend of my mother's. She had cut an ad from the newspaper, writing, "Carmen, I don't know if you saw this, but I thought it might be of interest." The ad was by a single writer offering book-writing services. I called her right away.

The writer was in her fifties and lived in Woodstock, a wealthier area of Vermont. She'd authored a book about being abused as a child. When I told her who I was, she said she'd followed my story in the *Valley News.*

"You're such an inspiration," she said.

"Thank you," I said. "I've been trying to write a book, and a friend's daughter is going to help me type it, but I'm not a writer and I need help organizing the material. Do you think you'd be interested?"

"Absolutely!" she replied. "I'd love to help you."

"The thing is," I said, wincing, "I don't have the money to pay you right away."

The woman didn't miss a beat. "Don't worry about it," she said. "We'll just see what happens." Before we hung up, she also told me that a friend of hers filmed documentaries and that she would put the two of us in touch.

I was on cloud nine. Things were happening. *I've got this going on now!*

We spoke one more time before Christmas, and she said she'd call me back the first of January to get started. When two weeks into the new year passed and I still hadn't heard from her, I called and left her a message. "Hi, this is Carmen," I said, hoping I sounded friendly and not pushy. "I just wanted to touch base with you. I know you're probably busy, but give me a call and let me know what's going on."

She never called back. She totally dumped me!

I was shocked. Was it about the money? I wouldn't have blamed her if she'd said she couldn't do it. I knew it was difficult for people to tell me no sometimes, but I wished they would be honest from the start rather than make promises they'd fail to keep. After so much excitement about finally moving forward with my book, I was back at square one. At least I still had Michaela. I gathered all my handwritten pages and put them in the mail for her. Then I took my next steps toward speaking.

I got the idea to join Toastmasters when I was researching public speaking online. The organization was a nonprofit that helped people improve their public speaking skills, and there were several chapters in my area. I asked Kess to give me a ride to White River for a meeting.

"Toastmasters? That's to learn how to speak in public, right?" she asked.

"Exactly."

"You know, I think I'll go with you," she said. "I need to do these education classes for work, and I should get better with speaking."

The meetings were held at the Veterans Administration in White River, and the group had about a dozen members. A few women were doing it to build confidence. Others needed the skill for work. Everyone was there to improve, and they didn't take it lightly.

The meetings were very structured, following the same formula each time. We were given a book with ten to twelve speech topics in it, and we gave those speeches in order. The atmosphere was serious and professional. Though my natural inclination was to socialize and joke, I settled into the routine and worked as hard as everyone else. The only hiccup was that I couldn't see gestures or facial expressions; I also sometimes had trouble hearing with my one ear! In such moments, I had to lean over to

Kess and whisper, "What are we doing?" For the most part, however, I kept up and reveled in actually being out of the house, doing something new.

Most of the meetings began with a category called "Table Talk." Each week, somebody was assigned to develop a topic for the next meeting; then that person would randomly choose a member of the group to speak extemporaneously on that topic for two or three minutes. When I was picked, it was surprisingly easy to speak without preparation. Not seeing people's faces lessened the anxiety, the way it had when I was on the stand for Herb's hearings, and I liked the challenge of entertaining on the spot. Maybe I was more ready for this than I'd thought.

My only concern with Toastmasters was that its goal was to make speakers very polished. I didn't want to sound rehearsed. I wanted to be genuine and authentic, the way I was during Table Talk, even if that meant I sometimes stumbled on my words or took a second to calm my emotions. I sensed that my speeches would be more powerful that way.

My excitement with doing Toastmasters—that fervor to do something new—also led me to take karate. My mom's boyfriend, Marshall, ran a school in his basement. He had told me months earlier, "Come to the dojo anytime you want to try it," but I'd put it off because of my tissue-expander surgery. Now I thought, why not? I had always been a tomboy, playing softball, digging in the garden, and carrying thirty-pound bags of mulch. My movement was limited, but I was ready to do something physical again—or at least try. I knew Marshall would let me do the best I could and not push me further than my body would allow.

I started karate in January, and my mother and Kess joined at the same time. Maybe they were inspired by the fact that I was putting myself out there and doing new things; why couldn't they?

In the beginning, Marshall did a private class with just Mom, Kess, and me. He led us through a twenty-minute warm-up that called for jumping jacks and floor stretches. As Mom and Kess leaned forward, grasping their knees or ankles, I could only move my torso a few inches; I just looked like I was sitting there. Then Marshall called for twenty sit-ups and twenty push-ups; they kicked my ass. It would take me months to work up to that, but I was game for trying. After that, Marshall showed us some basic punches and blocks.

After a few private sessions, we felt comfortable enough to join a class with other people. The kids' classes ended just before the adult ones began, and in the minutes before ours started, we all milled around, chatting and catching up. For the first time in years, I felt as if I were part of the community again.

Classes alternated between teaching self-defense with our arms and our legs. I cringed when the kicking bag made its bi-weekly appearance. The nerve damage in my left foot shot pain from the sole all the way through my leg when my foot made contact with the bag. After a while, I just pretended to kick it, my foot stopping short of the synthetic leather.

Once I got home from each class, I realized the full toll karate took on my body. I was starting to suspect that my neck surgery back in September had failed; the scars were bulging again, and my neck was so tight that it pulled me forward and put stress on my back. I enjoyed karate, but I cried after each class. All I could do was hope it would get better.

Meanwhile, our Toastmasters class was busy with people giving their "Icebreaker" speeches. The topics were general, meant to help us get to know one another. One lady had just lost her job and explained that she was taking the class to increase self-esteem. My own Icebreaker speech was scheduled for the second week of February.

With all this build-up, I was anxious to get behind a podium. Except for the feelers I'd already put out with local organizations, I didn't know where to start. That was where Marshall stepped in again.

"Why don't you speak at the dojo?" he asked. "People already think what you're doing there is inspiring. Tell them why you're doing it. You can call your contacts at the *Valley News*, and we can make flyers and advertise."

I felt a surge of pleasure that Marshall would do that for me. "That sounds great! Let's do it."

My mother said, "You know, I bet the Fairlee Church would love to have you come out and speak. Why don't you give the minister a call?"

I took Mom's advice, and the minister soon came to my house to meet me. "We've been praying for you for years," he said. "Ever since you got hurt. I'm so happy that you're feeling better. What would you like to speak about?"

"Well ...," I said, "I was thinking about forgiveness."

"Forgiveness?" His voice lifted in surprise. "What about it?"

I lifted my shoulders slightly into a shrug. "I've forgiven Herb for what he did, and it's made an enormous difference in my life. I think it would be nice to share that with your congregation."

"Well, Carmen, that would be lovely. How about Sunday the twelfth?"

We put it on the calendar, and when it was later moved to the nineteenth, I realized that my schedule that week was filling up: I had my Toastmasters Icebreaker speech two days after the Fairlee Church and Marshall's dojo only a day later. It was going to be a speaking baptism by fire.

CHAPTER 20

LIVING
OUT
LOUD

KNOWING I WAS GOING TO SPEAK ABOUT FORGIVE-
ness made me remember a question Mark Davis, the
Valley News reporter, had asked me earlier: "Does Herb
know you've forgiven him?"

"No," I said, caught off guard. "I hadn't thought about it."

Now I was thinking about it. If I was going to share my
forgiveness with others and encourage them to forgive,
maybe it made sense to share it with Herb as well. I was no
longer stuck in my pain. I felt wiser, as if everything had
happened for my benefit: what could *I* learn from these
experiences? How could *I* use them for positive change?
Herb had made a choice that stripped him of his freedom—freedom I'd recovered through forgiveness. Maybe
he was at a point where knowing of it could help him.

In early February, I contacted Amy, a victims' advocate
for the state prison system. She was the one who had told
me of the reporter trying to talk to Herb, and she was
the one who arranged contact with prisoners. I asked
her now if it would be possible for me to talk to Herb.

"Why would you want to do that?" she asked over the
phone.

As I held my cell phone to my right ear, I remembered Kess telling me when I woke up, "Carm, you don't have an ear." It seemed like a lifetime ago. I said to Amy, "Because I've forgiven him, and I'm just wondering if hearing that might do some good."

"Oh." She paused, as if not sure what to say. "Well, there's a process we need to go through before connecting you with him. I'll need to ask you a few more questions, and then I'll interview his therapist and other prison staff. We just need to make sure this isn't going to do more harm than good to either of you."

"I understand," I said. "How long do you think it'll be before you know?"

"Let me see how he's doing psychologically and I'll let you know."

° ° °

As the week of my speeches approached, my nervousness collected into a solid mass in my stomach. I didn't want long pauses or awkward silences. I didn't want to break down and cry. So, to practice, I talked into my tape recorder. I was alone in a quiet house, free to stammer, pause, and take breaks when I needed them.

When I was done, I played the tape and listened carefully. My voice was not the voice I'd had before the attack, but it was strong. I noted where the speech stalled or meandered and edited those areas in my mind. Then I recorded it again. I did that two or three times, enough to feel comfortable with the *order* of my speech but not enough to memorize it. I wanted it to be cohesive, not perfect.

On Sunday, February 19, my mother and Marshall came

to pick me up for the church service. My mother was flustered, talking fast and firing questions. "How are you feeling, Carm? Are you sure you're up for this? Do you want to go over your speech in the car? You sure you know what you're going to say? You're going to do great."

"It'll only be ten or fifteen minutes, Mom," I said, inwardly rolling my eyes but smiling at the same time. Her mother-hen concern was comforting in its predictability, but the truth was that she wasn't the only one who was anxious. The closer we came to Fairlee Congregational Church, the quicker my breath came. By the time we walked up the steps of the old, beautiful white wooden building, my hands were trembling.

Mom, Marshall, and I slipped into a row, and Mom smiled and waved to people she knew.

"Carmen, we're looking forward to hearing you speak," the woman next to me whispered, squeezing my hand.

After the first part of the service, when the minister would ordinarily give a sermon, he called me up to the stage. "I'd like for us all to welcome a very special guest today," he said. "For those of you who don't know, Carmen Blandin grew up in our area. Four years ago, she was hurt by someone she loved and trusted. Carmen asked to speak to you all today about a very important topic: forgiveness. Let's all give her the welcome she deserves."

The audience clapped thunderously, and my heart pounded as I stepped toward the stage. The minister guided me to the microphone, making sure I was settled before stepping away. I squinted at the audience. A row of windows right across from me cast blinding sunlight over the congregation. I couldn't make out anyone's faces or even tell anymore where my mother was sitting.

"This is my first time speaking." My voice cracked, and I cleared my throat. "So I'm a little nervous."

Dead silence.

"But I hope you will bear with me. Most of you already know who I am and what happened to me—so I'm not going to focus on that. What I want to talk about instead is how I'm here standing in front of you. It's because of forgiveness."

I told them about last spring, how my scars had reddened and swelled, debilitating me so much that I couldn't leave the house. I explained how the redness had gone away during my surgery in June, when I was anesthetized and my mind was at rest.

"I thought it had something to do with not letting go," I said. "I thought maybe it was a physical manifestation of the heaviness I was carrying. So I decided to try to forgive as an experiment."

I talked about how I'd bought the audio books, how I'd listened to Louise Hay and *Embracing Change.* I told them how I'd revisited the good times of my marriage and how, without even realizing it, I came to forgive.

"And you know what? After I forgave, that redness never came back."

Did forgiveness have anything to do with how the swelling stopped? There was no way to know. We link things together, and there's no right or wrong answer if it gets us to the places we need to go.

"Now that I've forgiven Herb," I continued, "how can I not forgive someone for the little things? How can I hold a grudge against someone now when I let go of the biggest grudge I could ever carry? We don't realize how much negativity we hold onto. People hurt our feelings, or our family doesn't come through for us, and we hold the little slights along with the big ones. We carry them with us, and we get used to the weight. We don't realize how much lighter we could be if we let it go. Forgiveness is something we do for ourselves. It is the key to finding happiness."

I stopped, thinking back to my tape recorder in the kitchen. I imagined its shape in my hand, hearing my voice resound in the quiet house. Had I said everything I wanted to say? Was I forgetting anything? No. I felt satisfied that I'd shared the message I wanted to share.

"Thank you for listening," I said.

The church filled with applause, long and loud. I was immensely proud of the step I'd taken toward my future.

After the service, we stayed around for refreshments, and I talked to anyone who wanted to talk to me. I was milling beside my mother when a man approached me.

"Carmen, I don't know if you remember who I am," he began.

I stepped close enough to him to see his face. He looked exactly as he had when we'd gone to Fairlee Elementary School together, more than thirty years earlier.

"I know who you are," I said. "Your name is Shane."

He laughed. "That's impressive. Look, I just wanted to tell you that I really enjoyed your talk. There's this thing I've been dealing with for a long time—someone hurt me, not in the same way, but they hurt me—and I've been holding onto it for more years than I can count. I don't know if I'm able to forgive, but I'm going use your talk to try."

Shane's words suffused me with warmth. My talk had inspired someone. "All you can do is try," I said. "I really hope it works for you."

243

o o o

I was exhausted for the rest of that day, but there was little time to rest. I had my Icebreaker speech in two days and my speech at Marshall's dojo the night after that. The Toastmasters speech would be straightforward; according to our book, I was to share something personal about myself and explain why I had joined the organization. I put more thought into what I would say at the dojo, especially since Marshall had been getting a strong response to his flyers and ads.

When I thought about that speech—and any speech after that—I tried to anticipate the questions people wanted to ask but were uncomfortable voicing. Those were the toughest subjects to address: disfigurement and blindness. I wanted to make sure I could do it without breaking down.

Tuesday night's Icebreaker speech passed without incident. I stood before the group and told stories about when I was a kid. I told them I was born and raised in the Upper Valley and that I'd gone to nursing school and then moved to LA. I explained that I was there because I wanted to share my story with people on a big level. Like Eileen had said, I wanted to use this opportunity to help more people than I ever could as a nurse.

By the next day, I was overwhelmed but also inspired. I had come so far in one year, no longer trapped in the darkness of my physical limitations and emotional pain. Even if I couldn't speak full time, the way regular people could, I knew this was something I wanted to pursue. My intuition had been right.

Fifty people crowded the dojo when Kess and I arrived that evening. Mom, who lived with Marshall, was already there, and Liza and Hannah came together later. Some people in the audience were dressed in karate *gis*, like me, from an earlier class, but most wore regular clothes; they had come specifically to hear me speak. Adam Sullivan, the TV reporter I'd worked with in the past, was there with his camera, and Jen was there to take photos for the *Valley News*. As everyone settled into the folding chairs Marshall had arranged, I took a seat at the front of the room.

For the next twenty-five minutes, I spoke mostly about disfigurement. "It never bothered me until I heard that graphic warning," I told them. "I knew it was worse than I thought—worse, even, than just being damn ugly!"

People laughed.

"But the thing was that once I started feeling bad about it, it changed the way others responded to me."

I told them about the little girl crying on the bus and how I felt like a monster for a while. I paused for a moment, feeling tears rise to my throat. *You're strong, Carm*, I coached myself. *You've got this.* I explained how the day came when I broke with the burden of feeling so miserable about the way I looked and the way things somehow changed after that. It was as though I'd released years of pain, past and future, in one afternoon of bitter weeping. Slowly, I said, the more comfortable I felt about who I was inside, the more accepting I became of the way I looked outside.

"No one has reacted negatively to me since then, child or adult," I said. "In some way, changing my perception about myself affected everyone else's perception of me, too. The energy we put out there matters."

When I finished speaking, I invited the audience to

ask questions.

"What was it like to look in the mirror for the first time?" someone asked.

"It was more than difficult. More than painful," I responded. "Words can't describe what it felt like to look in the mirror for thirty and forty-five seconds at a time and not see yourself. I couldn't *see* myself. We identify our face with who we are, and it was unbelievably strange to look in the mirror and think, 'How can that be me? It doesn't look how I feel.'"

"Why did you go back to the same house?" another woman asked.

"We needed to take our power back," I said, "and claim the home as our own. He took away so much that it felt important not to give him that, too. Anyone else?"

"Are your kids here?" a lady asked.

"Yeah, where are they?" I tried to crane my neck. "Put your hands up, girls!"

Liza and Hannah embarrassedly raised their arms, and I introduced them to the crowd. "My mom and sister are here, too," I added.

Afterward, everyone lingered at the dojo to chat and enjoy refreshments. I saw Adam interviewing several people, including Hannah, and Jen snapped photos as she walked around. She took one as my fifth grade teacher and elementary school principal, now a couple, approached. I hadn't seen them since I was a kid, and my old principal hugged me close. Jen's camera flashed. The picture would be in the next day's *Valley News*.

"Do you remember when all the teachers got together and played that prank on me?" my old principal asked, laughing.

I laughed, too. The teachers and bus drivers had plotted not to take us the full way to school one morning. They stopped at the post office down the road, so that the principal was the only one at school. The kids were saying, "We want to go to school," while the teachers replied, giggling, "Wait a minute, just a few more minutes."

"Do you remember, Carmen, you were always in his office, bugging him all the time?" teased my old teacher.

"What can I say?" I said, laughing back. "I really liked him. He was funny."

"Well, I liked you, too," he said. "And it's wonderful to see you doing so well."

After we hugged good-bye, a tall man with a mustache and beard approached me. He was one of the men in the ambulance with me that night.

"I'm really glad you made it, Carmen," he said. "It certainly didn't seem like you were going to."

"Thank you," I said. "And thanks for coming to see me."

I appreciated having people be strong and curious enough to come out and talk to me. I believed I was on the road to changing not only my world, but other people's worlds as well, just by being me. I thought, *This has to be the best life in the world.*

° ° °

In early March, as promised, Amy called me back. Her voice was shaky when she said, "I've spoken to Herb. I'd like to come over and tell you in person what he said."

Amy knocked on the door later that week while Hannah was at school. She was thin and in her mid-forties, with curly brown hair. We walked together to the living room and sat down.

"So," I said, "you talked to him?"

Amy took a deep breath. "It was the strangest thing. He started out very friendly. 'Does Carmen want to talk to me? Does Carmen want to see me? I'll do whatever I have to do.' Then he got paranoid. 'I might lose my TV privileges if I go to Vermont, but I'll do it if she wants me to.'"

"Well, that sounds positive," I commented.

"Wait. I'm not done." Amy paused. "He wasn't remorseful, Carmen. He didn't take any responsibility for hurting you."

My heart jumped, just for a second. "What do you mean?"

"He said he asked God for a signal not to hurt you. He waited until his birthday, but he never got anything. He thought that must mean God approved of his plan. He said that if he didn't hurt you," Amy said softly, "his soul would evaporate."

I was silent as Amy's words sunk in. I remembered my little voice telling me to call him that night, after the girls went to bed. But I didn't know how to listen to myself. I didn't know how to identify that voice as my own intuition, a part of me that was more aware than the conscious me. I don't think most of us know how to do that; some don't hear the voice at all. If I had listened—if I had called him and wished him a happy birthday—would he have taken that as a sign not to hurt me? Would he have thought that was a voice from God telling him to dump the lye, turn his truck around, and forget the whole horrible idea? Or would it simply have postponed the inevitable?

"Is that all?" I asked.

"It sickened me, Carmen," she said fiercely. "It's not right.

I had to go for a walk just to try to shake some of it off."

"It's too bad," I said. "But, look, if you ever hear that he's better, that he's taking responsibility, let me know. I am more than willing to help him with my forgiveness."

Amy stared at me for a moment. "Sure, Carmen. I'll do that. Listen … there's one other thing I wanted to talk to you about while I'm here."

She told me that National Crime Victims' Rights Week was in April and that the Vermont State Prison was holding an event called Place at the Table. The victims' rights advocates were arranging a table with a place setting and photo of an area crime victim, most of whom had been murdered. Prisoners would be let into the room to read the victims' stories and listen to speeches from survivors and family.

"Would you be interested in speaking?" she asked.

I was floored. I hadn't done anything like that before, but it sounded like it could be powerful. Maybe I could help people.

"Yes," I said. "I'd like that."

"Oh, that's great, Carmen!" she said, bursting into a wide smile. "I'll let you know over the next month what we need from you. Thank you!"

After Amy left and I had the house to myself, I sat on the couch and peered inward. How was I feeling about Herb's lack of remorse? I was *surprised*, yes. I couldn't understand how he didn't regret his actions and wondered if it was because he didn't fully know what I looked like. If he could run his gaze over my whole body, take in the damage that he'd done, he'd have to regret his actions, wouldn't he? Ultimately, it didn't matter. He was sick, and his lack of remorse didn't upset me. Neither did it influence my forgiveness; that was independent of him. I realized something profound then: forgiveness was more than a choice. It was more than strength or courage; it was more than me, more than anything I could do. It was a gift.

CHAPTER 21

FACING FORWARD

MY SPEAKING CALENDAR FILLED UP QUICKLY.
By the end of March, I was booked to speak twice a week
at different venues all the way through May. I didn't
allow myself to worry whether I was doing too much
too soon, even though my physical discomfort seemed
to be increasing. After my neck surgery in September,
I had anticipated being able to get off my pain medication. From December through February, I had weaned
down to one-third of my usual dosage, but by April I was
terribly uncomfortable. I could feel the thick bands of
scars thickening on the right side of my neck. My mother
confirmed: "It doesn't even look like you had anything
done now, Carmen." I'd need to call Dr. Pomahac soon,
but my immediate focus was on my next speaking en-
gagement: National Crime Victims' Rights Week at the
Vermont State Prison.

The speech was on a Wednesday in mid-April, and I
had no idea what I was going to say. What did prisoners
want to hear about? What did they *need* to hear about?
What could I share that would actually help them, not
just contribute to a cycle of guilt or self-loathing? On
top of these questions was the knowledge that Herb had
been held at that prison for a year and a half. Some of

the people I'd be speaking to probably knew him. They probably knew parts of the story—and parts of Herb—that I never would.

Amy picked me up in the morning for the forty-five-minute drive. She glanced at me from the driver's seat as we merged onto the interstate. "How are you feeling? Do you know what you're going to say?"

"I'm nervous," I said. "And, no, I don't. Are there any guidelines?"

"No guidelines. Just go up there, be yourself, and say what you're comfortable saying."

For the rest of the drive, she explained how the day would unfold. The prisoners would be led into the room and read the victims' stories before the speeches began. Besides me, another nurse—who had been hit by a drunk driver—would speak, as well as a woman whose son had been murdered in the early nineties. There would be a morning session, followed by lunch, and then an afternoon session.

We reached the prison around ten, and I followed Amy to a big open room. There was an anticipatory bustle as the victims' advocates set up the table, arranging photos and belongings before each seat. My place setting was at the end of the table. There was a framed photo of me with my bio, as well as a picture of me with my girls before the attack and one after. A friend of mine named David, who had contacted me after reading one of my newspaper articles, had made me a wooden bowl that I let Amy use for my place setting.

The other nurse, Barbara, was there when we arrived, and soon we were making small talk about our careers. I told her I'd worked at Hitchcock and UCLA, and she told me she worked in the mental health field. She'd followed my story in the papers, she said.

We waited an hour for a group of a dozen prisoners to be led inside the room. Slowly, they walked around the table. Some of them let their gazes linger on the photos while others passed more quickly, as if not wanting to confront the victims' faces. Eventually, they all dropped onto the folding chairs that had been set up on one side of the table. The murmur in the room hushed as their attention turned toward us.

We spoke in what seemed to me an ascending order of crimes: first Barbara, who had suffered more emotional trauma than physical; then me, with my extensive injuries; and then the third woman, whose son had been murdered.

When it was my turn, my nervousness felt like a blood rush to the head. I thought it was more because I didn't know how to address this specific audience than because this audience happened to be prisoners. I didn't feel scared to stand before them or among them. I simply wasn't sure what to say. Concisely, I explained what had happened to me and told stories about the challenges I'd overcome with disfigurement and blindness. The blue jeans I was wearing chafed against my scars as I spoke.

After I sat back down, the third woman went up and talked about her son. She was in her sixties or seventies, and her voice reminded me of the woman at the World Burn forgiveness session—the one whose anger was still a spark in the room, ready to ignite. My heart ached for her. It had been twenty years since her son was killed, but the pain in her voice was as raw as if it had happened yesterday. I couldn't imagine living with that kind of anger for so long.

The session passed quickly, and a large group of us went to a pizza and sandwich place five miles down the road for lunch. I ordered a turkey sandwich, pleased at the normalcy of sitting around a table with others and chatting about our morning. I overheard the older woman and her family talking to one of the victims' advocates; one of the men arrested for killing her son was getting out of prison. She cried angrily about how unjust it was that he was being released when her son was still gone. Again, I saw with clarity that she had not yet healed.

Lunch lasted for quite some time as we waited for more prisoners to be driven in from other parts of the state. By the time we returned—minus the older lady, who had left—my legs were throbbing and the scars on my neck were pulling my lip down and making me drool. I distracted myself by thinking of what I could say in my next speech. It would be a new group of inmates, all sex offenders. What could I say to them?

Back in the room, I was shocked at the difference in turnout: a hundred prisoners in bright, different-colored jumpsuits filled the folding chairs. Amy had said the group would be larger, but I'd never expected this many people! My anxiety about trying to say something that would benefit them increased. I didn't want my speech to be another guilt trip: "Hey, I'm a victim, and you guys suck." They had been hearing for years how they should have thought differently and acted better; how would they ever break their own cycle if all they heard was how guilty they should feel for it? I wanted to do something different. I saw this speech as an opportunity to lessen the pain in the world.

My stomach jumped as I walked to the front of the

room. Even as I stood before the arrangement of chairs, I had no plan except to be honest—to be me. As I opened by telling them what had happened to me, I couldn't help a shiver of unease; which of these men had known Herb? What had Herb told them about me? That I was a bitch who deserved what I got? What did the prisoners think about me? I shook these thoughts off as best I could. I was here to do a job, and I wouldn't do it right if I let myself get caught up in questions whose answers I'd never know.

For the next twenty minutes, I spoke more about blindness and disfigurement, revisiting the places of struggle that felt at once so close and so distant. Toward the end of my speech, I said, "I'm determined to overcome my challenges. I've overcome a lot already, but I know I have a long way to go ... physically and emotionally. Just because I look like this doesn't mean I don't want a relationship some day. It doesn't mean I don't want to fall in love. Don't you guys want to fall in love some day?"

I paused. There was quiet movement in the audience.

"Do any of us want what has happened to us or what we have done hanging over our heads forever? Preventing us from being the people we want to be? I'm not going to allow what happened to me to limit the rest of my life. You shouldn't, either. Thank you for listening."

Amy asked for questions, and a few orange-sleeved arms rose. I picked the first one I saw.

"Have you forgiven him for what he did?" a man asked. I could hear an inflection of hope in his voice.

"Since I got hurt," I said, "I've realized that anybody who hurts another person has been hurt themselves. We are all victims of victims. So am I all that different from you? I don't think so.

"Yes, I've forgiven. The thing is, you don't necessarily need your victims' forgiveness. You can't focus on what you have no control over, letting that dictate how you feel about yourself. You need your *own* forgiveness. You need to take responsibility for your own health and wellbeing. That's how you'll get to a point where you'll never hurt someone again."

Another arm jutted out from the crowd, and the voice that accompanied it was young. "I never forgave my perpetrator," he said. "I was treated the same way I treated my victim. I didn't forgive, and I just repeated the cycle. What if my victim does the same?"

I repeated my first answer. "Your only goal is to help yourself, not your victim. That is what I truly believe. 'Selfish' is a bad word in our society, but I think we're not nearly selfish enough. We never put ourselves first the way we should. I thought I did, but I didn't, either. And when I say selfish, I don't mean in a malicious way. I mean taking *care* of yourself as your first priority. Because unless you do that, you can't fully take care of anyone else. Forgive yourself first. Then see what other changes come."

I realized the truth of my words as I spoke them. As a society, we self-sacrifice to our own detriment. Women are especially bad about this. We work hard, we raise our children, we're exhausted, and we keep saying yes when someone asks for another favor. We don't say, "I need a night to myself." We don't say, "I'm sorry—I can't take an extra shift this weekend." We accept responsibility for other people's happiness before we accept responsibility for our own. If we reversed that, we would be better mothers, better spouses, and better friends, siblings, and daughters.

Women could take a cue from the men in their lives—husbands who say, "I'm playing golf this Sunday," or "I'm watching the game tonight." We can, and *should*, call for the same balance. We should ask our partners for help so that we have time for a girls' night or a massage. Women are so accustomed to helping men that we don't know how to accept help in return, and many men don't know how to offer it. Women have the power to change the world, especially when it comes to violence. If we *own* that power by teaching our husbands and sons the emotional intelligence that comes naturally to us, it can change everything.

I was the last to speak that afternoon, and afterward a couple of prisoners came up and thanked me. One older man said simply, "I'm trying to forgive myself for what I've done. Thank you for making that feel okay."

Amy gave me a ride home, and fatigue pushed me deep into the seat. My whole body pulsated with pain. By the time I was able to remove my jeans, the scars on my butt and the backs of my legs were beginning to swell. I touched them with surprise; they hadn't done this in a year—not since before I'd forgiven.

Exhaustion and physical discomfort aside, I lay in bed that night feeling better than I had in years—perhaps ever. I was putting myself first, the way I'd described to the prisoners, and doing something I'd been waiting to do. For the first time in my life, I was convinced that I was on the right path and that it was going to have the far-reaching positive effect I'd sought. I had also finally, fully, accepted my disfigurement. This was different from the day I'd cried the year before. This was a deep, peaceful recognition that I looked the way I looked and could use it to my advantage.

I called Dr. Pomahac the next day and left a message for him with Hilary, one of his assistants. I told her that my scars were acting up and that my neck was bothering me again. On a late Friday afternoon, my phone rang.

"How are those scars doing?" Dr. Pomahac asked.

"Much better," I said. "The redness on my legs went away rather quickly this time. I think they just acted up because I wore jeans. But I don't know what's going on with my neck. I think we need to do something else, because it's getting all tight again."

"Well, I'm calling to talk to you about something else, actually."

There was a tone to his voice I hadn't heard before—a conspiratorial excitement.

"Okay …," I said.

"You've had such open wounds that I haven't felt it was appropriate to say anything before now," he said. "But now that they've healed … you know I've been doing face transplants? It was on the news this week."

"Oh, right," I said politely, lying. *What is he talking about?*

"I'm not saying you're a candidate," he said. "We'd have to do extensive testing. But if you *are* interested, you could really benefit from a face transplant."

"Okay. Well, what would it do?"

"You could potentially have blinking eyes and a fully functioning nose and mouth," he said. "But the biggest benefit for your quality of life, Carmen, is that it would replace those scars on your neck."

I ran my fingertips across the tight bands of scars above my collar, the ridges that dipped and rose and caused so much pain. I touched my nose, feeling how my nostrils were caved in on one side, and then my lips, which never fully closed. I imagined being able to have a conversation with someone without the embarrassing drooling and slurping. I thought of being able to *blink*, that most natural human function that I had been missing for four years. If I could blink, I could better preserve my artificial cornea. I could be rid of the drainage and discharge I still had to clean from my eye every morning and could leave my ubiquitous tissues behind.

"Would my Medicare cover it?" I asked.

"No. I've gotten a grant from the Department of Defense to do five patients; I've done two so far. The grant covers all the tests to determine whether you're a candidate, as well as the surgery itself and your care for up to three months after." He paused. "I know there's a lot to consider. I just want you to think about it. I'm going to send you more information next week, but feel free to call me with any questions."

My head was spinning as I hung up the phone. A *face transplant*? Was that exactly what it sounded like? I was a nurse and hadn't even heard of such a thing. And what timing! Right before Dr. Pomahac called, I had a path. I was out speaking, I was continuing to work on my book, and I was finally using my disfigurement to my advantage. I felt good about myself. Now, suddenly, I had the option *not* to be disfigured? What did this mean?

The first thing I needed to do was learn more about face transplants. Over the next hour, I read that the first partial face transplant had occurred in 2005 and the first full-face transplant had been performed the previous year. Dr. Pomahac had completed the first U.S. full-face transplant in March—just two months ago—on a Texas man who had lost his lips, nose, and eyebrows in a power line accident. In all cases, the face transplants were exactly as the name implied: a donor matching the patient's gender, blood, and tissue type gifted the patient a face. The face would change over time to fit the patient's bone structure; in the end, patients didn't look like the donor, but neither did they look like themselves. They might resemble a sibling or cousin.

Evening fell as I sat at my iPad, zooming in on before and after pictures online. They were stunning. Men and women who had been mauled by wild animals, shot by spouses, and burned in fires went from wearing veils and living in solitude to rejoining society. They were able to smell again, to speak and taste food, to blink and interact with the world. Their new faces may not be traditionally beautiful or look one hundred percent "normal," but they were an unimaginable improvement. A new face could give a person new life.

As much as I saw the benefits to a face transplant, I was overwhelmed with the science-fiction enormity of it. I would have someone else's *face*—someone who had lived and loved and, by nature or tragedy, died. I remembered a black and white movie I'd watched as a kid, in which a double agent changes his face to look entirely different by the end. I'd thought with horrified fascination, *My god, this man is wearing someone else's face!*

On the other side of it, knowing that someone's family was going to give me their loved one's face was terribly moving. I had been an organ donor from the time I was old enough to drive. I was not attached to the *idea* of my body; after I died, someone else could take what they needed. The thought of being on the receiving end of something as personal as a face felt like the biggest, if strangest, gift.

After my initial research, I made a mental list of pros and cons. The first con was that I would need to go through considerable testing. Each trip to Boston was exhausting, so I would have to stop speaking in order to pursue something I wasn't even sure I could have. I didn't know how long it would take to determine whether I was a candidate and then, if I were, how long I'd need to wait for the surgery itself. For an unknown period of time, my life would be a waiting game. Then, of course, was the seriousness of the surgery itself; assuming (as I did) that there were no complications during the operation, how long would it take me to recover? How successful would the operation be? What if I ended up no better, or even worse, than where I was now? There was no doubt that this would be a long ordeal.

On the pro side, if it worked, I would have a mouth that could kiss, a nose that could breathe, and blinking eyes that could save my sight. I would be able to travel and speak without struggling with the pain in my neck, which would open all new doors for my future. Those things were everything to me. Aesthetics were almost a complete afterthought. If looking like everyone else was the only or biggest pro on the list, I would decline the surgery. The thought made me recognize how completely I had accepted my disfigurement—just in time to weigh another option.

When I called my mother and sister to tell them, they were just as conflicted as I was. ("Someone else's *face*? That's so creepy, Carm!") But when I explained the pros and told them to look up before and after pictures online, their discomfort turned to excitement. "You could have a new face!"

Liza was away at college, but Hannah was home that weekend. She looked at me incredulously when I told her about the surgery.

"Well, you're not actually going to *do* it, are you?" she asked, blue eyes wide.

"I know it's a big surgery, but I'm not afraid I'll die," I told her, though she hadn't said the words. "It's not a concern of mine, so I don't want it to be a concern of yours. It's just—imagine if you had my face, and you couldn't smile or kiss, and people didn't know when you were crying or laughing. But the big thing is blinking eyes. I want to save my sight for as long as possible. And the neck—oh, the neck!"

After a few moments, Hannah nodded. "I can see why you'd want to do it, Mom," she said. "It's just weird, thinking of you with a different face."

"I know, honey. It's weird for me, too."

After a few weeks of weighing the pros and cons, I realized that my mind was made up: even if I wasn't ready to commit to the surgery, I had to pursue the possibility.

∘ ∘ ∘

I went to Brigham in June to officially start the testing process. In addition to seeing Dr. Pomahac, I would be meeting with the entire transplant team, as well as psychologists, physical therapists, speech therapists, and occupational therapists. If everyone agreed I was a good candidate, I would begin the more invasive physical testing. That was, I figured, the point of no return. Until then, I would move forward as though I'd already decided to do it, and I would see how it felt.

I had an idea to film a documentary, so I asked my mother to bring a video camera with her the first time we went to Brigham. I knew it would be all over the place, but the doctors spoke freely and I was excited to capture these beginning phases.

First I had to speak with a psychiatrist on the face transplant team. She asked me to tell her my story, including why I was interested in a face transplant. She must have wanted to make sure I was approaching this decision from a stable place. I talked to her for an hour about my recovery, my family, and forgiveness.

The next psychologist was independent of the transplant team. She asked me detailed questions about my moods: what had my general mood been like in the last seventy-two hours? Was that different than in the last two weeks? Was I on any anti-depressants or anti-anxiety medication? I told her I had taken Xanax for a year and a half before stopping and that I felt more positive than ever since then. I told her I'd been going out speaking and how fulfilled that made me. I explained that my goal was to help people on a big scale.

After a month of visiting with the psychiatrist, psychologist, and half a dozen other doctors, I returned to see Dr. Pomahac.

"Everything has gone just fine," he said. "Now is the time to decide whether this is what you want to do."

It was July, only a year since he had put the tissue expander in my back, at a time when I'd had no idea such things as face transplants existed. "I've gone through the process this far waiting to see if I had second thoughts," I told him. "So far nothing has come up. I'm ready to take the next step."

As expected, the process was exhausting. For each trip to Brigham, I woke up at a quarter to six and my mother picked me up by six thirty. We drove half an hour to the bus station in Lebanon for the two-and-a-half-hour ride to Boston. Then we walked to the street level to hop a taxi to the hospital. After spending all day getting MRIs and CAT scans, having blood drawn and other tests run, I caught the four thirty bus to arrive home by seven thirty. The trips were all-consuming.

Once I started physical testing, the hospital issued a press release about my face transplant. Erin, the senior vice president of public affairs, also told me she'd put the word out that I was looking for a documentarian. One day, at the gym, she overheard a woman mention film production on the phone. When the woman hung up, Erin introduced herself and told her my story. It turned out that the woman was an author, journalist, and documentary filmmaker. She had directed documentaries for PBS and Discovery Health, and she had contributed to dozens of other major networks. She had even been nominated for an Emmy. Erin was bubbling with excitement when she told me that the woman, Jody, was interested and wanted to talk to me.

She called in mid-July, and we spent some time getting to know each other on the phone. Jody was slightly older than I was and lived outside of Boston with her husband and four-year-old son. When she told me she wanted to film my documentary, I felt a sense of déjà vu. "I'm practically bankrupt," I said. "I can't pay you. We would have to arrange something for after the documentary is done—profits or royalties, I'm not sure how it works."

"I understand," Jody said. "I really want to do this for you. We'll figure out compensation."

From that point on, Jody and I emailed regularly, and she made several trips to the Upper Valley to film me speaking. She also accompanied me to Brigham for testing. I couldn't wait until this was all over and I could see the footage arranged in some kind of order. I'd also be able to use it to write my book.

Just as I thought things couldn't get busier, I received an unexpected call as a result of Erin's press release: I was invited to appear on a national television show.

CHAPTER 22

LET
IT
GO

THE DOCTORS SHOW ON CBS. NATIONAL TELEVISION. I had worried that pursuing a face transplant would pause the rest of my plans. Now it seemed I was hurtling forward, with the opportunity to reach hundreds of thousands of people at one time.

The show's producer, Joni, asked me to travel to LA in September to film the segment, which would air the following month. She informed me that I'd be sharing the spot with another woman who had received a partial face transplant.

"I'm sorry," I said. "I'm not interested in that."

I wanted to share my story without people subconsciously associating it with another, I explained. Joni seemed to understand, and she agreed to change the lineup.

The week before I was scheduled to leave, one of the film producers came to Vermont with his crew to get footage for the show. They came to my house first and then to my mother's to interview her and Kess. My neck discomfort had worsened, so I chose to stay home while they did the interviews.

What I didn't know was that they would use a certain technique to reveal me on the show. They would ask Kess to tell the story of what happened, and the footage would play right before I was brought on stage. My family knew I never answered questions about that night, nor did I want anyone else telling my story. When the producer asked Kess about it, she said, "I don't know if Carmen wants me to say."

"Oh, I've already talked to Carmen," he said. "It's okay."

I hadn't answered that question, though. As I'd told Joni, I wanted to tell the story on my own terms.

That night Mom, Kess, and I went out to dinner at an Italian restaurant called Stella's in Lyme, New Hampshire. My cell phone was out of service range, and when signal returned, I had one new voice message. It was the field producer, letting me know that he was thinking about contacting the chief of police to request the 9-1-1 tapes from that night.

I called him back, my voice raised with indignation. "No, you are not going to do that!" I said. "Those are my *daughters* on that tape."

"I was just asking," the producer said mildly.

"No, you were not 'just asking,'" I shot back. "You were telling. You were going behind my back, and I am not happy about it."

To the producer, I probably seemed overly frustrated, overly sensitive—and I was. My story was my most guarded possession. I had no power to change what had happened to me, but I *could* control how I shared it and with whom. Any time I felt someone pulling at those threads against my will—taking away my control—I lashed out. My trust was frayed.

Between frequent trips to Boston for testing and working with Jody on the documentary, the weeks passed quickly. Soon it was September, and Jody called to tell me she couldn't go to California as planned; she was juggling a heavy load and couldn't work the trip in. I assured her it was fine, as the producers were going to give me film anyway.

Then, twelve hours before I was set to leave, Kess called. She was crying.

"I think I told them too much," she said.

"What do you mean? I'm sure you did fine."

"No, Carm. I got so caught up in the questions, and I was overwhelmed with the cameras ..."

I gripped the phone tighter. "What did you tell them?"

"Everything."

"*Everything*?" I repeated. "Damn it, Kess, why would you do that?"

Kess wept softly over the phone. "I'm so sorry, Carm."

My mother and Kess had done more interviews than anyone in my family had, and I always told them that if they shared how they felt about *their* experience, I would never get upset. I simply asked that they never try to speak to *my* experience, just as I would never presume to speak to theirs.

"Kess, I don't want to say anything I'll regret. Just give me some time."

When we were younger, Kess and I used to fight about nothing and go without speaking for months on end. I didn't want to do that anymore. I had changed. But I still needed space to cope with losing the only thing in years I'd been able to control: my story.

It was almost six in the evening when Kess and I hung

up, and Mom and Marshall and I were slated to leave at four-thirty the next morning. I choked back my feelings of anger and panic and forced myself to think clearly. *How important is this?* I asked myself. *Is it important enough not to go? Your story is going to be shared one way or another. You're just being controlling because it's the only thing you feel you have control over. But the truth is that it doesn't really matter, does it, if Kess tells most of it and not you?*

I realized that if I was going to be in the public, in the media, I had to learn to control what I could and let go of the rest. Could I have controlled more in the situation and prevented this? Yes. I could have chosen to go to my mother's house for their interviews—but I didn't. Now the only choice to make was whether or not to do the show. And if I did, what was still left for me to control?

I called Joni and explained what had happened.

"Look," I said, "I understand why they asked Kess about what happened, and I know Kess didn't mean to reveal so much. But if she repeated anything that my daughters said or experienced, I'd really like to cut that out. Is there anything we can do?"

Joni was caring, warm, and understanding of my feelings. She stayed up with me until midnight, trimming the edges from the story Kess had told. Of course, I couldn't change everything—and what I couldn't change, I had to let go.

∘ ∘ ∘

My mother, Marshall, and I arrived at our hotel at ten o'clock the next night. It been a long day of travel, and I slept hard in the hotel bed. By the time I knew it, it was five a.m. and the alarm was ringing.

I dressed in nervous excitement, and Mom, Marshall, and I went down to the little coffee shop in the lobby. We waited, cardboard cups in hand, for a car to pick us up and deliver us to the studio.

Though I was still anxious, I let myself enjoy the sheer fun of the day. Who ever thought I'd be on national television? I picked at the food they'd set out for us in the dressing room and flicked through a rack of clothes they'd pulled for me. (I was supposed to bring an outfit of my own, but I'd forgotten it.) I chose a pair of black pants and a black tank top, with a scarlet-colored sweater and headband. The room bustled as producers and hair and makeup people rushed purposefully in and out. I was signing paperwork, sipping coffee, and catching up with my younger sister, Rachel, who lived in LA and had met us at the studio. She was twenty-eight, and I hadn't seen her since the previous November. The whole morning had an atmosphere of excitement and celebration.

It wasn't until just before I went on stage that my nerves hit full-throttle. They had wired me with a microphone, and I waited at the back of the stage while they prepared for me up front. *What if it's too much for me to hear my story this way?* I thought. *Well, I can't do anything about it now. Let's just see if I can get through this.*

Dr. Travis started talking about me on stage, and then my own pre-recorded voice rang out. "My name is Carmen. I'm a mother of two daughters. I'm also a daughter myself. And also a sister." I knew that interspersed with my words were photos of me before getting hurt: smiling, smooth-skinned, beside Liza and Hannah, laughing with Kess and my mother. "No one can imagine how much a life can change in just fifteen minutes."

270

I was walked onto the stage, where I stood in darkness beside Dr. Travis. A large screen filled my vision. I couldn't make out all the detail, but I could see my sister's serious brown eyes as she began speaking.

"It was around two thirty in the morning," Kess said, "and Carmen's ex-husband had a ten-pound weight and tied a rope around it. He swung it into a sliding glass door and entered the house."

Piano music played in the background as Kess spoke, and the screen alternated between showing her face and zooming in on black and white images of my house. Over the next few minutes, Kess related the story that I had guarded so fiercely for four years. *Let it go, Carm*, I reminded myself.

"I saw Carmen lying on the bed," Kess said. "She was intubated. She was unconscious. She was almost completely wrapped up, like a mummy."

The screen switched to show my mother, her eyes watery. "My first thought was that I was in the wrong room," she said. "I had the experience of falling down a hole. I realized I had gone to hell."

"The flesh that was burned and exposed was either red or brown or starting to turn black." Kess's voice cracked. "The doctor explained as best he could what he was seeing. I leaned forward in my chair and asked, 'Do I need to go in there and say goodbye to my sister?' He said, 'The chances are more likely she won't survive.'"

"The nurses were also talking about Carmen not surviving," my mother added. "I said, 'You guys forget something. She has two daughters. If there's any way she is going to make it, she's going to make it.'"

The piano music faded as my family's images stilled

on the screen. I was shaking beside Dr. Travis, my heart pounding. The audience was impossibly silent.

"I'd like for you all to meet Carmen," Dr. Travis said to the audience. "Go ahead," he said to me, softly. "Turn around."

I was on the verge of crying but choked the tears back. *Take a deep breath. Crying defeats your whole purpose.*

Long, loud applause rang in my ears as Dr. Travis walked me a dozen feet from the screen to two white chairs. It was just enough time for me to regain my composure.

Unsteadily, the first thing I said was, "I am really nervous."

Dr. Travis smiled warmly. "You don't have to be."

"Okay, I won't be then," I said, making him laugh. After that, I was fine.

For the next hour, we filmed four segments of the show. First we talked about what happened that night and then afterwards—how I had chosen to live.

"Carmen, when you're lying there," Dr. Travis said, "and you had to make a choice, how did you choose between life and death?"

I told him about my dream. "Every word flashed on a screen. Life. Is. A. Choice. I feel very strongly that I chose to stay."

We talked about the obstacles I'd overcome, how I was out speaking, how I'd forgiven, and what my future looked like now. At the end of the show, Dr. Travis video-conferenced Dr. Pomahac to talk about my face transplant. Finally, Dr. Travis told the viewers that my injuries had brought me financial hardship and that I was being added to the Dr. Phil Foundation. He encouraged donations from anyone who wanted to help. I had received so much over the years—so much generosity and love and support—that I hated to ask for more, but I reminded myself of one of the first lessons I'd learned: *Be open to receiving. Be appreciative. Give back how you can.*

"I'm going to tell you right now, Carmen," Dr. Travis said, leaning toward me and touching my knee. "I've seen a lot of stories of resilience in my career, but I've never seen someone more resilient than you. Ever."

The audience cheered as I rose to hug Dr. Travis. He hugged me back tightly, kissing my cheek. I wasn't sure how much of what we'd discussed would actually air, but I felt good. I'd had fun and experienced a world I never could have anticipated entering. This was a step toward the big future I saw for myself.

° ° °

I didn't talk to Kess for a week. Finally, I wrote her an email: *Okay. I'm over it.*

We say that a lot: I'm over it. I needed time to make sure it was true before I said it. I didn't want to jeopardize my relationships by pretending to move forward when I hadn't. By the time I pressed Send, I was confident that I had let it go.

Later, Kess told me, "I got this feeling like I shouldn't have been talking. I just—I don't know why I did it."

"Next time listen to your gut," I said. "That's all I can tell you."

My own gut was taken by surprise a few days later when I received a call from Jody, my documentarian. Hannah and I had moved out of our old home and into an apartment earlier that month. I could no longer pay

273

the mortgage and was working with a pro bono attorney to reach an agreement with the mortgage company. The house was technically still mine, though, and I had invited Jody to film me there. We would walk from room to room as I told the story. A week before she was scheduled to arrive, she said, "I'm sorry. I just can't do it anymore. I bit off more than I can chew, and I need to stop."

Immediately, I burst into tears. *Again?* This was happening *again?* Aside from the idea of my book, I was most excited about the documentary and so grateful that she was donating her time to help me. But on the phone, she was matter-of-fact. I saw that there was no changing her mind, nor would I have tried.

I let myself cry for a few minutes after we hung up; there is no worse disappointment than *surprised* disappointment. When I thought about it, though, I realized the writing had been on the wall the whole time. She had a young son and was teaching at the university level, as well as running her production company. I knew she cared about me and for my story, but ultimately other commitments came first. People had the best intentions when they agreed to help me. What they didn't understand was that I preferred an honest no to an uncertain yes from the beginning.

It just wasn't meant to be, I told myself. *Let it go.*

If the documentary wasn't going to happen, I would focus my energy on writing my book. I realized now how big an undertaking it was; I wasn't a writer, and—as I'd discovered—I couldn't even put pen to paper for longer than fifteen minutes at a time. But I'd find a way.

° ° °

A few weeks after my episode of *The Doctors* aired, Joni told me they wanted to video-conference me back on.

"We want to tell you how much money has been donated so far," she said, a smile in her voice.

"Can you give me a hint?" I asked.

"No. All I can say is that it's big."

I waited out the next few weeks in excited anticipation. I had no concept of what "big" might mean and hardly dared to hope for what I needed. My debt was an enormous weight that I didn't know how to ease.

In mid-November, my mother drove me to Kess's apartment because she had cable TV and Internet. We set up the computer *The Doctors* had sent us and followed Joni's instructions to see the show they were taping that day. Dr. Travis was sitting in a semi-circle of stools among several other people, and he recapped my story for the audience. Then he asked, "Carmen, do you want to know how much people have contributed so far to the Dr. Phil Foundation in your name?"

"Yes!" I exclaimed. "I would love to know."

They chuckled, and my heart pounded.

"So far," said Dr. Travis, "eighty-six thousand dollars has been contributed."

There was no air in the room. The audience cheered and clapped, and I felt about to burst. I wished my face could express my excitement and gratitude. "Thank you so much, everyone," I said, pressing a palm over my chest. "Thank you so much. It means so much to me."

"We've had such an outpouring to your story," Dr. Travis said. "Thank you for showing us what it means to be resilient."

It would take weeks for the money to arrive, and in

the meantime I heard from Dr. Pomahac: he and his team were ready to present my case for candidacy to the hospital's ethics panel. They were the ones who would review all my test results and Dr. Pomahac's research in order to give final approval.

On December 5, after six months of testing and evaluation, my name was officially added to the face transplant list. At the time, less than two dozen others worldwide had undergone the procedure.

"Congratulations," Dr. Pomahac said over the phone. "Now it's just a matter of time—you can be called at any point next year."

I wanted to push him for more details—was "any point" more likely to be early in the year or later—but I reminded myself to be patient. *Watch your life unfold*, I told myself. *Remember, patience isn't just waiting. It's understanding that life is going to happen as it happens, and you can't push against it. You can only open yourself to receiving what it brings.*

° ° °

After paying off bills and putting money aside for the girls' education and our living expenses, I tucked the rest away for a special use: to write my book. Then I splurged on a special Christmas for Liza and Hannah.

For the first time since being hurt, I was able to give my girls exactly what they wanted: new iPods for both, a BlackBerry for Hannah, and spending money for each. Liza was home from college, and the two of us went to my mother's house on Christmas Eve for dinner. (Hannah had to work, so we would return with her the next day.) All night, we sat and ate and laughed among the rich smells of baking turkey and ham.

The next morning, the girls and I stayed home as we always did. Kess came over early to cook breakfast, and she was a flurry of activity in the kitchen as she cracked eggs over the pan and peeled potatoes for home fries. The scents wafting from the kitchen were warm and familiar, inviting the rest of us to poke fingers into the food before it was on plates.

After we ate, we padded back into the living room to open presents. Everyone plopped onto couches, chairs, and the floor as we passed gifts back and forth. I still filled stockings for my girls, and they always teased that the loot wasn't very good—too much candy and gum, too little of anything else. "If you're going to do stockings, put real gifts in them," Liza said, laughing. "You should wrap them, too."

"I'm blind!" I objected.

"You always use that as an excuse."

I laughed. "I know, I love it. Fine—I'll get you better gifts, but I'm not going to wrap them."

This year I had enough sight and felt well enough to do my own Christmas shopping. I reveled in choosing unique little gifts for the girls' stockings—cute Lands' End key chains for both and a small trivia book for Liza—as well as the requisite candy and gum.

"These are *much* better," the girls said, grinning as they pulled the gifts from their stockings.

With my family surrounding me, I felt that no one had more to appreciate than I did. A string of colored lights shone from the six-foot Christmas tree Marshall had cut from his property; it was the tip of a larger tree, and the branches were awkwardly curved, sticking straight up. I called it our Charlie Brown Christmas tree, and everyone noticed the beautiful, brightly colored owl ornament right in front. All my Santas—skinny, fat, plush, porcelain—stood on top of the wood-burning stove we never used, and a few Christmas cups held candy that had dwindled as the season wore on. I gazed at the tree, which I had so yearned to see for years. I couldn't distinguish the sparse little branches, which I knew weren't very pretty. I only saw the lights that sparkled so cheerfully.

Life had been simple before I got hurt, and I had not known how to appreciate its beauty. I had not known how to truly live in the moment, appreciating each tiny gift as it came. Now I knew. I was awake and aware, and my heart was full of gratitude. My life was mine to create.

And I *really* looked forward to creating the rest of it.

ABOUT THE AUTHOR

Born in West Fairlee, Vermont, Carmen Blandin Tarleton worked as a nurse in Lebanon, New Hampshire, for nearly eight years before relocating to Los Angeles in 1996. She joined UCLA as an RN, working 12-hour shifts as a single mother of two daughters. She began dating Herbert Rodgers—a soft-spoken, well-liked hospital vendor—in 1998, and they married three years later in 2001. In 2003, while still at UCLA, Carmen founded CNH Legal Nurse Consulting, offering her expertise to attorneys on both sides of medical malpractice suits. When Carmen and her family moved back to Vermont in 2006, she resumed her nursing career at Dartmouth-Hitchcock Medical Center.

After a nine-year relationship—much of which was happy—Carmen and Herb separated in January 2007. Five months later, with no history of violence in their relationship, Herb broke into Carmen's home, beat her with a baseball bat, and soaked her with industrial strength lye. Carmen burned from the inside out. Her injuries were so severe that, hours later, only her hands and teeth were recognizable to family. Chances of her survival were grim; predictions for her quality of life, if she did live, were even bleaker. Doctors induced a coma, and Carmen endured 38 surgeries over her three-and-a-half-month sedation. When she awoke in September 2007, she was blind and disfigured.

After spending three years simply surviving (Carmen has undergone more than 55 surgeries), she realized her purpose: to counter the negativity Herb put in the world with her own positivity. Carmen recognized that by sharing her story, she could help people on an even broader scale than she had as a nurse. She could help them see that, no matter their situation, no matter what suffering they have endured, their reservoirs of strength are endless. They can choose to live. They can choose to find happiness, forgiveness, and peace.

Carmen began speaking in public in February 2011. Since then, she has spoken at fundraisers, domestic violence groups, classrooms, rotary clubs, and the Vermont State Prison, where she addressed an audience of convicted sexual offenders. Through her new path, Carmen has found the deep joy and self-fulfillment she sought her whole life.

Carmen's story—and her message of perseverance—has captured major media attention, with featured pieces in the *LA Times*, MSNBC, Fox News, *Reader's Digest*, *Washington Times*, and the *Boston Globe*, among numerous other outlets. She has also appeared on Emmy-award winning show *The Doctors*, receiving $80,000 in donations for medical and other expenses through the Dr. Phil Foundation. In December 2011, Carmen was approved for a face transplant, only two dozen of which have been performed worldwide. The 17-hour surgery is slated for 2013. Carmen hopes it will put the simplest actions—such as blinking—within her reach again, giving her greater freedom to fulfill her purpose: inspiring people to truly live.

Carmen currently lives in Thetford, Vermont. Her two daughters, Liza and Hannah, are thriving in college. Carmen is open to whatever the future holds for her.

HOW THIS BOOK
WAS CREATED

Carmen Blandin Tarleton's indelible *Overcome: Burned, Blinded, and Blessed* is the result of heartfelt collaboration between Carmen and the Round Table Companies (RTC) storytelling team. To create this book, RTC executive editor Katie Gutierrez and director of author support Kristin Westberg conducted a series of intensive interviews with Carmen over a period of several months, using those to help craft the book you now read. Throughout the process, the book touched the hands of RTC's writers, editors, proofreaders, transcriptionists, designers, and executive team. We are grateful to Carmen for inviting us into her journey, for bravely revisiting heartrending memories, and for sharing so authentically how happiness can come from struggle. Carmen is an extraordinary spirit, a force that entered the lives of the RTC team and changed them all. It is our hope that in reading this book, you felt the energy of everyone who contributed to its creation. We also hope you felt as though Carmen was speaking as directly to you as she did with us.

www.roundtablecompanies.com

CPSIA information can be obtained at www.ICGtesting.com
Printed in the USA
LVOW101510050313

322834LV00019B/422/P